SECRET
MONTREAL

SECRET MONTREAL

The Unique Guidebook
to Montreal's Hidden
Sites, Sounds, & Tastes

Tod Hoffman

WITH PHOTOGRAPHS BY
Linda Rutenberg

ECW PRESS

THE CANADA COUNCIL | LE CONSEIL DES ARTS
FOR THE ARTS | DU CANADA
SINCE 1957 | DEPUIS 1957

We acknowledge the support of the Canada Council
for the Arts for our publishing program.
This book has been published with the assistance
of grants from the Ontario Arts Council.

CANADIAN CATALOGUING IN PUBLICATION DATA

Hoffman, Tod
Secret Montreal : the unique guidebook
to Montreal's hidden sites, sounds, & tastes

Includes index.
ISBN 1-55022-311-9

1. Montreal (Quebec) – Guidebooks.   I. Title.

FC2947.18.H63 1997   917.14'28044   C97-930537-3
F1054.M83H63 1997

Maps prepared by Rita Bauer.

Design and imaging by ECW *Type & Art*, Oakville, Ontario.
Printed by Imprimerie Interglobe inc., Beauceville, Québec.

Distributed in Canada by General Distribution Services,
30 Lesmill Road, Don Mills, Ontario M3B 2T6.

Distributed in the United States by Login Publishers Consortium,
1436 West Randolph Street, Chicago, Illinois, U.S.A. 60607.

Published by ECW PRESS,
2120 Queen Street East, Suite 200, Toronto, Ontario M4E 1E2.

http://www.ecw.ca/press

PRINTED AND BOUND IN CANADA

TABLE OF CONTENTS

INTRODUCTION

This book will appeal to a unique sort of traveler. Explorers, really. Those who aren't content to collect exactly the same pile of snapshots taken from exactly the same spot as every other tourist. Those who instinctively — with disdain, even — turn left when they see a tour bus turning right.

Secret Montreal will show you the less traveled Montreal, that which is often neglected even by native Montrealers. We'll turn over some stones on your behalf and peek underneath. We'll lure you off the beaten path to help you discover your own. As a result, your trip will be a far more rewarding adventure. No matter whether you've visited the city several times, or whether you live here, *Secret Montreal* will take you to a city you've never seen before.

Montreal's greatest asset is its diversity — a vibrant blend of European attitude spiced by a multi-ethnic character. Within the space of a few blocks, you can encounter restaurants and boutiques boasting treasures from every continent.

Despite the anxiety many Quebecers feel in relation to their political future, visitors will not sense a pervasive doom-and-gloom attitude. The city remains lively and culturally active. Although a declining English population means that major theatrical productions and concert tours often ignore Montreal in favor of larger centers, the city's indigenous artistic life continues to thrive in a manner unique to us. Foremost are the multitude of summer festivals, while the local literary and sports scenes also hold much interest.

Too many visitors confine themselves to the downtown core and Old Montreal. While these areas are not to be missed, if you don't venture beyond, you'll never take in the city's true richness, which waits to be discovered in all its variety throughout the island. *Secret Montreal* will steer you in the direction of lesser-known delights. From there, you can take in the sights and sounds that make this city a cultural jewel.

One of Montreal's great advantages is its relative safety, not an insignificant concern for tourists today. That's not to say that the streets are crime-free. Of course they aren't. But explorers need not imagine themselves to be restricted to some previously trod course. Montreal is a marvelous city in which to meander aimlessly.

Secret Montreal does not offer prescribed tours or itineraries. Organized by subject, this book is intended as a guide for setting your own itinerary according to your personal interests. There is something here for everyone. I hope that *Secret Montreal* will open up a city you would otherwise have failed to see, and introduce you to things you would otherwise never have thought of doing. Enjoy the book, and use it to enjoy Montreal to its fullest.

HOW TO USE
SECRET MONTREAL

Entries in *Secret Montreal* have been organized alphabetically by subject. This allows you to look for sites and attractions that appeal to your particular interests. To help you maximize your time, we have included several useful maps. Each covers a section

of Montreal to which this book is likely to entice you. Entries
such as museums, monuments, public buildings, and churches are
accompanied by numbers corresponding to their map locations.
Once you've decided what interests you most, use the maps to
organize your days. A place name written in italics means that the
location is mentioned elsewhere in the book. Use the subject index
to find all relevant references. A second index is organized numeri-
cally according to map entries. This will help you find entries
quickly if your preference is to arrange your outings by district
and you want to be sure not to miss any of the nuggets to be mined
just around the next corner.

A note regarding the directional references is called for. Boulevard St. Laurent divides Montreal into east and west. Addresses
begin counting up in both directions from this street, commonly
known as the Main. Therefore, the higher the number you're
looking for in either direction, the farther you go from St. Laurent.
The St. Lawrence River marks the southern extremity of the city.
When you are directed south, go toward the river; when you are
sent north, move away from the river. Keep this in mind, and you
should always be able to navigate smoothly.

OTHER
RESOURCES

No tour guide, prepared months before it hits the book stands, can
hope to include all the transient attractions, exhibitions, shows,
and so on that pass through the city over the course of a year. To
know what's on at the galleries, museums, theaters, and clubs

during your stay in Montreal, consult the following periodicals, all of which are widely available.

The *Gazette* is Montreal's venerable English daily newspaper. Its roots can be traced to American publisher and statesman Ben Franklin. When Franklin returned to the United States in 1776, following his brief sojourn in town, he left behind his printing press, which was put to use by *La Gazette du Commerce et Litteraire*, a French paper that debuted in 1778. It eventually became a bilingual publication, and then entirely English. Each issue of the current *Gazette* has a "Show" section with entertainment listings. Friday's paper has a "Preview" section with extensive weekend highlights. The Saturday edition, which is the equivalent of the Sunday paper in most American cities, has an expanded "Entertainment" section. Daily issues cost 57¢, Saturday $1.75. The *Gazette* can be found at all newsstands and in any corner grocery store, known locally as a *dépanneur*. You'll also find it in white vending boxes on street corners.

The *Mirror* and *Hour* are free weekly papers issued every Thursday. They publish underground news, alternative viewpoints, and, most importantly, the most extensive and eclectic entertainment listings possible. Search here for information about the alternative music scene, the unconventional bar and club scene, the ostentatiously non- (even anti-) commercial art and gallery scene, as well as assorted restaurant and café reviews. Both papers are widely available. Seek them out in street-corner vending boxes and on racks in most magazine stores, pharmacies, record shops, coffee shops, smaller restaurants, and an eclectic variety of other retail outlets.

Voir is for those interested in partaking of the French entertainment scene. It is the French equivalent of the *Mirror* and *Hour*, but will contain listings that might not be found in the English papers. Find it wherever its English counterparts are distributed.

Montreal-Scope is a monthly digest format magazine styled after the indispensable *Paris-scope*. Between its listings and ads, it is comprehensive and helpful.

InfoTouriste is the official tourist information office, conveniently located in the heart of downtown at 1001 Dorchester Square, at the corner of Metcalfe, just south of Ste. Catherine (tel: 873-2015, or from outside Montreal 800-363-7777; Metro: Peel). Open 08:30 to 19:30 June 1 through Labor Day, and 09:00 to 18:00 Labor Day to May 31, InfoTouriste can supply reams of info on Montreal and the rest of Quebec, assist with hotel bookings and car rentals, and generally direct you to mainstream attractions throughout the city. It is sold in most magazine shops.

SECRET
AFRICA

Being one of the great North American venues for artists from French-speaking Africa, Montreal is a hotbed of African culture. For two weeks each July the **Festival Nuits d'Afrique** (tel: 499-9239) has the city swaying to its infectious rhythms. Among the clubs taken over by the festival is **Club Balattou** (4372 St. Laurent, south of Laurier, tel: 845-5447), which features worldbeat artists all year round.

Artefact International (200 Laurier West, suite 375, west of St. Laurent, tel: 278-6575) is a store that could pass for a museum. It stocks distinctive, crudely evocative carvings, jewellery, and magnificent drums from all across the African continent.

Giraffe (3997 St. Denis, south of Laurier, tel: 499-8436) is more accessibly priced than Artefact. The collection of objects is correspondingly less spectacular, but still contains some treasures.

For a taste of Ethiopia, try **Au Messob d'Or** (5690 Monkland, west of Girouard, tel: 488-8620; Metro: Villa Maria). The restaurant is open for dinner only, and the cuisine is considered authentic.

SECRET
ANTIQUES

❖

Antique stores have a tendency to cluster. In Montreal they have done so along a stretch of Notre Dame West between Atwater and Guy (Metro: Lionel Groulx). Conveniently, you can commence or end your browsing at *Marché Atwater*.

Grand Central (2448 Notre Dame West, tel: 935-1467) is among the largest, with a grand collection of decorative lighting and furniture.

Ambiance (1874 Notre Dame West, tel: 931-6722), as its name suggests, specializes in atmosphere. In addition to selling antique treasures, it has one of the most delightful tearooms in town. And if you like an eclectic service in your own home, whatever you see in the dining room is up for sale.

Les Villages des Antiquités (1708 Notre Dame West) is like the shopping mall of antique dealers — ten different shops are housed here.

SECRET

ARCHITECTURE

Montreal boasts the largest collection of Victorian row-house architecture in all of North America. Mostly three-story walk-ups with unique external staircases, many are elegantly appointed with turrets and spires. You can't fully appreciate a walk along Montreal's streets unless you look up. At street level, many of these structures have been taken up by small storefronts and provide little aesthetic appeal. But look to their summit and you will see remarkably delicate attention to the detail of design. Also, take care to look for the outstanding stained-glass windows that were the rage for wealthy home owners in the 1800s. Among the streets where this architecture prevails are **St. Joseph**, **St. Hubert**, **St. Denis**, and **de Lorimier**. **Christophe Colombe**, directly across from *Parc Lafontaine*, also has some wonderful examples. ❷

There were three principal reasons why the outdoor staircase was adopted:

(1) It was a way for the city to hike property taxes — an internal staircase would signify that all three floors were part of a single structure, whereas an external staircase allowed each floor to count as a distinct dwelling with a separate address.

(2) Having an internal staircase wastes heat by sucking precious warm air up through the space occupied by the stairs.

(3) More space was afforded the ground-floor home because none had to be set aside to provide access to the higher floors.

Around 1940, the outdoor staircases were banned as an eyesore. However, seeking the advantages they offered, row houses were later constructed in the same manner, but with a partial brick wall to internalize the stairs. Excellent examples of this construction are to be seen along Sherbrooke to the east of *Parc Lafontaine*.

SECRET
ART DECO

Located in *Old Montreal*, the **Aldred Building** (507 Place d'Armes) is the quintessential art-deco structure. It was built in 1929, before the Empire State Building in New York took the style to its pinnacle. Don't just stare at the outside, but venture inside to see the light-enhancing stained-glass window, the sumptuous fixtures, the polished brass, and all the attention to detail that marked the craftsmanship of the era. (Don't ignore the 10-story building at **511 Place d'Armes**, right next door. Its distinctive red-brick construction and intricate wrought-iron portico are now dwarfed by the Aldred and the other modern towers that have virtually removed its profile from Montreal's skyline. But when built in 1888, this edifice stood proudly as the city's first sky-scraper.)

The **Sun Life Building** (1155 Metcalfe, north of René Lévesque; Metro: Peel) was for many years the largest building in the British Empire. Built between 1913 and 1933, it was the headquarters of the Sun Life Assurance company until they fled Montreal in 1977, soon after the election of the province's first separatist government. Again, don't just gawk at the exterior, go in and gawk at the art-deco detailing and check for the periodic exhibits that are hosted in the lobby. ❹

Ever have a dream where you're dining on a luxurious cruise ship only to find yourself nine floors above urban concrete? Well, here's the place to live the fantasy. Modeled in the art-deco style of the stately *Île de France*, the **Eaton's ninth-floor cafeteria** (677 Ste. Catherine West, between McGill College and University, tel: 284-8411; Metro: McGill) has long been a favorite escape at the core of the city. It's rather pricey, but try it for lunch or a midday shopping break, or just peak in to have a look. ❺

SECRET
BASEBALL

Baseball fans should begin their tour at *Olympic Stadium* (4545 Pierre du Coubertin, corner of Pie IX, tel: 252-8687; Metro: Pie IX), the crumbling, tarp-shrouded, concrete behemoth that the **Montreal Expos** have reluctantly called home for the past 20 years. The best thing about watching a game in this echo chamber is that attendance has been so low most seasons that excellent seats can be purchased on game day. In his collection of essays *Home Sweet Home*, Mordecai Richler proclaims the Olympic Stadium the "largest, coldest slab of poured concrete in Canada." The Expos have been unfairly hampered by being housed in a terrible stadium, since the on-field product — not just the Montreal team, but major-league baseball in general — is wonderful. Ticket information can be obtained by phoning 790-1245 in Montreal, or 800-361-4595 from outside. ❻

The year 1996 was the 20th anniversary of the stadium and of Montreal's Olympic Games. Mayor Pierre Bourque marked the occasion with the unveiling of a five-ring commemorative statue on the Olympic grounds of Pie IX, near the corner of Sherbrooke. When most Montrealers think of the Olympics, it is not in the past tense, but in the present — as in, "How much are we still paying on the debt run up by the bloody thing?"

Montreal has a proud association with the grand old game of baseball. Foremost is Jackie Robinson's monumental 1946 season when he first broke mainstream pro ball's color barrier by playing for the Brooklyn Dodgers' AAA farm team, the Royals, who played at venerable **De Lorimier Downs**. The ballpark was inaugurated back in 1928, but it no longer stands; indeed, nothing stands to mark the old site, which is now in part a park (northeast corner of de Lorimier and Ontario). Jackie is fondly remembered with a statue outside the Pierre de Coubertin entrance to Olympic Stadium (this statue previously stood at the Downs) and with a blue number 20 — his old Royals uniform number — embossed in the turf on the playing field beside home plate. This latter tribute was paid during a ceremony prior to a 1996 game to mark the 50th anniversary of his year in Montreal.

Another bit of baseball history can be viewed at **Parc Jarry** (285 Faillon West, on the west side of St. Laurent; Metro: De Castelnau), the original home of the Expos (from 1969 until 1976). This wondrous bandbox has been refitted to serve full time as a tennis stadium, home to the annual Canadian Open (men and women playing in alternate years). It was a glorious place to watch baseball, having all the little quirks that are missing from the multi-sport, generic stadiums built in the 1980s.

Frappeurs (79G Brunswick, in Dollard des Ormeaux on the West Island, tel: 421-BALL; take Highway 40 west) is for those who love baseball so much that they've gotta take their own swings. Stand in the Frappeurs hitting cages and go to bat against mechanical pitching machines. A new feature is the baseball simulator, which promises to deliver the game like no video arcade ever could.

S E C R E T
BEER

Do you want to learn about how beer is brewed? More to the point, are you interested in tasting free beer? Looking for a novel way to increase awareness of their product, **Les Brasseurs GMT** (5585 de la Roche, on the small stretch just north of St. Grégoire, in the *Plateau Mont Royal* district, tel: 274-4941) decided to give free tours of its facility, including the opportunity to sample its award-winning brews. Established in 1988, GMT was Quebec's first micro-brewery. It began with Belle Gueule (a medium lager) and then added La Tremblay (a pale lager), La Canon (a robust, caramelly porter), and Blanche de l'Île (an easy-drinking white beer brewed from wheat malt in the German tradition) to their roster. Tours are guided by the brewers themselves, who are capable of explaining not only the hardware used in the making of beer, but also the recipes and ingredients that distinguish one from the other. The free tour and tasting takes place every Saturday on the hour at 13:00, 14:00, or 15:00. The visit takes approximately 45 minutes, and the rest of your stay can be devoted to tasting. Reservations are only necessary for groups.

SECRET
BIRDS

The forest on **Île des Soeurs (Nuns' Island)** (accessible off the Bonaventure Expressway, exit Île des Soeurs, or by following University south onto the Bonaventure access and exiting at Île des Soeurs; buses from Place Bonaventure) is a suburban oasis within five minutes of downtown. As you enter the island, you'll find yourself on Boulevard Île des Soeurs. Continue all the way to the end. At Hall Street you'll face the forest. Footpaths in summer and cross-country ski paths in winter traverse the area and offer a peaceful haven for birds. A favorite spot for Montreal's bird-watchers, it is recommended particularly for those experienced in the pastime because there are no guided tours to introduce the untrained eye to the species that frequent the island. However, for anyone anxious to escape the bustle of the city, Nuns' Island is a welcome refuge. If a walk in the woods isn't to your liking, then settle for a break at Parc Vancouver, situated beside Boulevard Île des Soeurs, for an unobstructed view of the St. Lawrence River and the South Shore. ❼

Summit Circle, the Westmount pinnacle of *Mount Royal*, is another site to which birders flock. Early morning is the best time to scan for birds, and members of the Quebec Society for the Protection of Birds gather there around 06:00 on Tuesday mornings in the spring for scouting trips.

Peregrine Falcon Information Centre (*Tour de la Bourse*, 700 Square Victoria, tel: 397-7400; Metro: Square Victoria), sponsored by Martineau Walker along with the *Biodôme* and *McGill University*, has been established to give people the opportunity to view the life of a pair of peregrine falcons that have been nesting since 1984 on the 32nd floor of the Stock Exchange Tower. Open from May until the end of June, accessible seven days a week, 24 hours a day, the center offers information on these noble raptors and a 55″ television monitor through which visitors can observe activity at the nest. ❽

S E C R E T

BOOKS

Complementing the mainstream shops, Montreal boasts several quirky bookstores that celebrate those works not destined for the top of the bestseller lists, as well as those that have already been there:

If you want to stock up on Canadian books while visiting Montreal, the **Double Hook** (1235A Greene, just south of de Maisonneuve in Westmount, tel: 932-5093; Metro: Atwater, Westmount Square exit) is devoted exclusively to them.

L'Androgyne (3636 St. Laurent, south of Duluth, tel: 842-4765) houses the most extensive collection of feminist, gay, and lesbian works in the city, as well as other titles.

Nebula (1832 Ste. Catherine West, east of Atwater, tel: 932-3930; Metro: Atwater) is the store for sci-fi, fantasy, and horror buffs.

The venerable **Word** (469 Milton, east of University, tel: 845-5640) is a favorite place for McGill students to browse for secondhand books.

Russell Books (275 St. Antoine West, east of Bleury, tel: 866-0564; Metro: Place d'Armes) is among the largest of Montreal's used bookstores, with a good selection of recent releases and rarer finds. Specializes in literature.

Argo (1915 Ste. Catherine West, east of Atwater, tel: 931-3442; Metro: Atwater) is cramped and musty, the way a used bookshop ought to be. Once you're browsing in the neighborhood, continue along a few doors west and drop in at **Westcott** (2065 Ste. Catherine West, tel: 846-4037).

This past summer, a brand-new **Chapters** megastore (1171 Ste. Catherine West, corner of Stanley, tel: 849-8825; Metro: Peel) threw open its doors to four floors of books, magazines, and a café. Is there any greater indulgence than to browse bookshelves while fortifying yourself with a frothy cappuccino? I don't think so.

SECRET
BREAKFAST

Picasso (6810 St. Jacques West, west of Décarie, tel: 484-2832) is the original home of the 24-hour breakfast. It's a favorite after-hours hangout for the late-night crowd who'd rather have their morning meal before going to bed. Very crowded at brunchtime on the weekends.

Eggspectations (198 Laurier West, west of St. Laurent, tel: 278-6411; and 1313 de Maisonneuve West, corner of de la Montagne, tel: 842-3447; Metro: Guy-Concordia) is upscale and trendy, yet the cooks don't refrain from serving mountainous portions, and the very friendly staff are always quick with the coffee refills, the only significant measure of a good breakfast spot. Open only for breakfast and lunch, into the late afternoon.

Restaurant Buymore (386 Bernard West, west of du Parc, tel: 270-3219) is a neighborhood fixture. Renowned locally for its breakfasts.

SECRET

BURGERS

This book may well stand as the only travel guide to mention a **McDonald's** (1 Notre Dame West, corner of St. Laurent in *Old Montreal*; Metro: Place d'Armes). But it's not for the food or the ambiance so much as for the historical import of the site. Among the great explorers who embarked from Montreal was Antoine Laumet de Lamothe Cadillac, who ventured southwest and founded the city of Detroit, before being appointed governor of Louisiana. The site of his birth on 5 March 1658, is now occupied by this McDonald's, where you will find a plaque and pictures of how the building looked before American fast food graced the interior. In exchange for permission to open at this location, McDonald's agreed to forgo their trademark oversized golden arches to achieve a better blend with the surroundings.

Yeah, so it's a long way to go for a burger, but eating at **Dic-Ann's** (on Pie IX at the corner of Castille, north of Boulevard Métro-politain, on the west side; Metro: Sauvé) constitutes a visit to a Montreal institution. Stop in for lunch before or after a visit to the *Olympic Stadium*, *Botanical Gardens*, or *Biodôme* — it's north of these attractions. The wafer-thin burgers with special BBQ gravy are one of a kind. They're cheap, but you gotta eat more than one. Sidle up to the lunch counter with the rest of the connoisseurs, or get a car order and eat in the lot. It ain't classy and it ain't listed by Michelin, but for all the fine dining we could do, this is how most of us eat.

La Paryse (302 Ontario East, between St. Denis and Berri, tel: 842-2040; Metro: Berri-UQAM) is proof that burgers can be more than just fast food. When they're as hearty and satisfying as the Paryse burger, they can be a meal. This cramped little snackbar is a favorite with students from the Université du Québec, right across the street. An ideal lunch spot, it's also a good place to grab a quick bite before a night on the town, as it's conveniently located just east of the St. Denis nightlife scene.

And don't forget **Mr. Steer** (1198 Ste. Catherine West, at Drummond, tel: 866-3233; Metro: Peel), home of the thick, juicy Steerburger. Treat yourself to an accompanying stack of curly, entangled Suzie-Q fries.

<h1 style="text-align:center">SECRET
CADAVERS</h1>

Strathcona Anatomy and Dentistry Building, McGill University. The third floor of this hulking brick edifice is the place for those who slow down for a close look at car wrecks. For here is where anatomy students — tomorrow's healers — happily hack and saw away at cadavers, all in the interests of science. Though probably omitted from the standard campus tour, there is a viewing gallery, and, since access to the building isn't controlled, you can creep up the stairs for a first-hand look (Strathcona is located at the upper eastern end of the campus, off University, south of des Pins; Metro: McGill).

SECRET

CAJUN

It's not surprising that French Canadians should relish the cuisine of their long-lost cousins to the south, and there are several Cajun kitchens for Montrealers to choose from.

La Louisiane (5850 Sherbrooke West, west of Girouard, tel: 369-3073), a cubbyhole of a place, serves up sizzling Cajun seafood, chicken, and pastas, not to mention all the classics: gumbo, po' boys, jambalaya, crawdads. Save room for their superb desserts.

Chef Michel, the original chef from *La Louisiane*, moved over to nightclub-cum-restaurant **Club Van Gogh** (2025 Drummond, tel: 847-5318; Metro: Peel) to prepare his Cajun creations. Enjoy a spicy meal in the lush dinner-club ambiance, and then work it off to the disc jockey or live band playing at the back on weekends.

Magnolia (5515 Monkland, west of Girouard, tel: 481-2020; Metro: Villa Maria) is the latest entry to the ranks of Cajun and Creole eateries. Cosy and inviting, it serves up a nice selection of Louisiana specialties. The blackened fish of the day is usually a good bet.

SECRET
CAVES

Tours of the **St. Leonard Caves** (Parc Pie XII, on Lavoisier between Viau and Lacordaire; take Boulevard Métropolitain east, Viau exit, Viau north to Lavoisier, and turn left; for reservations to visit the caves, call the city of St. Leonard at 328-8511, or Spéléo at 252-3006) are led by the Société Québécoise de Spéléologie (SQS) between May and August (admission is $5 for nonresidents of St. Léonard, free for residents). The only cave on the island accessible to visitors is around 35 metres long and contains fossils and calcified rock dating back 450 million years. First discovered in 1815, the cave was seen as something of a public hazard, but in 1980 it was opened by the city to permit visits under the supervision of the SQS. The tour of this unique geological feature takes around 40 minutes. Hard hats and lights are provided, and you are advised to wear old, warm clothes. There is also a 30-minute slide presentation on caves and speleology.

SECRET
CHEESE

La Trappe (1600 Oka, off Highway 344, tel: 514-479-8361; take Highway 15 north from Montreal to Highway 640 to Oka) is one of the oldest Trappist monasteries on the continent. You may tour the grounds of the monastery and visit its chapel for quiet reflection. Because of the monks' artistry, Oka cheese is world famous. Pick up a sample on your way from an *apple picking* outing or a visit to *Oka Park*. Situated just past the Lac des Deux Montagnes, northwest of Montreal, Oka makes for a pleasant excursion. **9**

SECRET

CHINATOWN

Montreal's Chinatown is small by the standards of Toronto or Vancouver, and it doesn't have any of those cities' awe-inspiring 1,000-seat dining rooms, owned by large Hong Kong chain restaurants. However, it is an old and exotic quarter. The Chinese were among the first immigrant groups in Montreal, and they staked out the portion of the Main (as St. Laurent is commonly referred to by locals) furthest to the south. More than just a concentration of Chinese restaurants, this is where Chinese Montrealers come to buy their groceries and household necessities like chopsticks and porcelain dishes, as well as Oriental fashions. Take the pedestrian walk along Boulevard de la Gauchetière, west from St. Laurent, and revel in the sights and smells of the district. **10**

The familiar Cantonese and Szechuan meals are available here, but why not try something different? Here are a few hidden tastes worth savouring.

Vietnamese immigration has lent its flavor to Chinatown in the form of soup restaurants. There are a couple along St. Laurent between Viger and René Lévesque, including **Crystal de Saigon** (1068 St. Laurent, north of la Gauchetière), a particular favorite. The meat- and fish-studded soups make a hearty meal, and are generally priced at under $5.

Meat pastries, either fried or steamed, are a Chinese delicacy to be found in many little cafés. For one of the best selections, try the grungy little **unnamed counter** on the ground floor at 52 la Gauchetière West, at the corner of Clark. The buns are inexpensive (under $2 each), so sample different varieties. Few non-Chinese venture into this establishment, so the waiters will be happy to explain to you the ingredients in each type. This is not the Chinese food you may be accustomed to, if you eat at Western-oriented restaurants. This is the real thing.

The **Jardin de Jade** (67 la Gauchetière, along the pedestrian mall, tel: 866-3127) is another great place for Chinese buns, available on the take-out side. There's also a sit-down restaurant.

Chinese desserts are usually omitted from restaurant menus, for some reason that remains unclear. But you definitely want to pass up at least one trip to the donut shop, and try some egg tarts, butter rolls, or custard buns instead. Get truly adventurous and order the sweet-bean or lotus buns. Any of these cakes can be found at the two places mentioned above.

Bring a sack full of these delicacies to **Sun Yat Sen Park** (corner of la Gauchetière and Clark). A small rock garden makes this unlikely corner rather peaceful, in welcome contrast to the chaotic scenes unfolding in the local shops and restaurants.

Johnny Chin is an artisan who practises the lost art of Chinese candy-making. Working from a stand he erects along the pedestrian stretch of la Gauchetière, he fashions delicate Dragon Beard Candy by hand. These morsels of cornstarch, peanut, coconut, sesame, and chocolate literally melt in your mouth. Dragon Beard Candy is native to northern China, but since the purges of the Cultural Revolution, few masters of this craft remain. After being captivated by the rhythmic stretching and rolling that results in the creation of each carefully fashioned candy, sample a piece for 50¢, or purchase a box of six for $3. The effervescent Chin, in the best tradition of the street-corner pitchman, keeps up a running patter that explains the history behind his candies, how he makes them, and what goes into them. You'll find him at work pretty much every evening between 18:00 and 20:30 from May until October.

Hungry vegetarians should see *Manho Restaurant* in *Secret Fruits and Vegetables*.

S E C R E T

CINEMA

Leo Ernest Ouimet's **Ouimetoscope** (formerly located at 1206 Ste. Catherine East) was North America's first dedicated movie palace when it opened in 1907. It no longer stands, but today's Montreal boasts the most cinemas per capita of any city on the continent, and this doesn't include the battered hulks of now abandoned classics like the York and Seville, which blight Ste. Catherine West between Atwater and Guy. Of the old, single-screen venues, only the grand Imperial (Bleury, just north of Ste. Catherine) remains in its original guise. The venerable Loews (Ste. Catherine West, between Mansfield and Metcalfe) is a five-screen multiplex, but the Loews 1 retains some of the glory from the golden era of cinemas.

There may well be a cinema like this in your town, but wouldn't it be a thrill to see an IMAX **Theater** (King Edward Pier, corner of de la Commune and St. Laurent, in the *Old Port*, tel: 496-IMAX; Metro: Place d'Armes) in the country where it was invented? Films are screened in English and French, so be sure to use the schedule to select a presentation you'll understand. The newest innovation in this technology is 3-D IMAX. It is absolutely stunning when applied to nature films or expansive scenery. ⓫

If you're a film buff, why spend an evening in a strange town watching a movie you can just as easily catch when you get home? For an alternative, check out the theater at the **National Film Board** (1564 St. Denis, south of Ste. Catherine, tel: 496-6887; Metro: Berri-UQAM), Canada's national film agency. It regularly screens films of the board's own making, or you can use Ciné-Robothèque to access the entire history of the board's productions. The NFB has won several Academy Awards, particularly in the areas of documentary, animation, and short subjects. Here's an opportunity to find out why. Open Tuesday through Sunday from 12:00 to 21:00. Adults $3 per hour, students and seniors $2 per hour.

Montreal's **Festival International des Films du Monde** (tel: 848-3883) is the city's best-known film event, now into its third decade. Held annually toward the end of August and boasting an array of big stars, it weans Montrealers off their outdoor summer festivals and acclimatizes them to the coming winter months when entertainment and shelter become their abiding preoccupations.

Cinemania, a festival of French films with English subtitles, entered its third year in 1996. It offers English-speaking film buffs the opportunity to see French films sans language barrier. Held for a week in early November at the Maxwell Cummings Auditorium in the Pavillon Jean Noel Desmarais of the Montreal Museum of Fine Arts (1380 Sherbrooke West, tel: 288-4200; Metro: Guy-Concordia). ⓬

Cinéma du Parc (3575 du Parc, north of Sherbrooke, tel: 287-7272) is a three-screen repertory movie house that serves up classic, foreign, and art films, as well as pre-video post-first-release movies.

Goethe Institute (418 Sherbrooke East, east of St. Laurent, tel: 499-0159; Metro: Place des Arts), the German cultural center, regularly screens German films.

SECRET CINE-MEALS

Café Ciné Lumière (5163 St. Laurent, just north of Laurier, tel: 495-1796) was inspired by the successful *Cité-Ciné* exhibit of several years ago. This cinema-esque restaurant lets you eat while sporting headphones that allow you to listen to the Super-8 classic being run on the screen. An ideal spot for solo travelers who normally feel uncomfortable dining alone. Brunches are a regular feature, and the various mussels and fries plates are worth a try.

Just when it looked as though the district around the old Forum would disintegrate with the hockey action moving to the *Molson Centre*, **Café Bistro Ciné Express** (1926 Ste. Catherine West, east of Atwater, tel: 939-CINE; Metro: Atwater) emerged, paying homage to the cinema. Popular with college students in the area, Ciné Express offers lunch specials at under $5. Sandwiches, pastries, a variety of coffees, and old-style sodas are on the menu, served in a homey, comfortable setting. At the back is a screening room where movies are viewed. Weekends feature live music, fashion shows, or stand-up comedy in the evenings. Call ahead to find out what's on the schedule.

S E C R E T
COFFEE BREAKS

Gourmet coffee is a much-savored pleasure throughout the city, and, in keeping with Montreal's French character, so is the venerable café. Everybody has their neighborhood favorite. Major chains such as A.L. Van Houtte and Second Cup are represented, but there are also several unique establishments.

Café El Dorado (5226 St. Laurent, north of Laurier, tel: 278-3333) serves good cakes, an original weekend brunch menu, sprout-laden sandwiches, and, best of all, coffees from every part of the world, including the incomparable Jamaican Blue Mountain.

Brûlerie St. Denis (1587 St. Denis, 3967 St. Denis, and 5252 Côte des Neiges) offers up an assortment of fine coffees at three locations.

Café République (5693 Côte des Neiges, 1051 Bernard West, and 6136 Côte St. Luc), another local chain that has spread recently, offers light meals along with assorted coffees.

La Petite Ardoise (234 Laurier West), a relaxing oasis situated in the middle of Laurier's stretch of trendy boutiques, serves lunch and brunch. If the weather's warm, try for one of the coveted tables in their courtyard terrace at the rear.

English traditions continue to flourish in Montreal's core, including the late-afternoon high tea. Two of the most elegant high teas can be had at **Ogilvy's** (1307 Ste. Catherine West, corner of de la Montagne, tel: 842-7711; Metro: Peel) and the **Ritz Carlton Hotel** (1228 Sherbrooke West, corner of Drummond, tel: 842-4212; Metro: Peel).

SECRET
CRAFTS

Café Art Folie (5511 Monkland, west of Girouard, tel: 487-6066) gives you the opportunity to have a coffee while creating your own ceramic artwork. Over 100 undecorated ceramic pieces are on sale

($4 to $50). Select the one you want, and Art Folie will provide you with paint, brushes, and stencils, not to mention advice, so you can decorate it to your taste. In addition to the price of the piece, you pay for however long it takes you to complete your creation ($8 per hour, or $5 for children under 12 and seniors over 60). The cost includes glazing and firing (this requires three or four days, so allow enough time to collect your masterpiece before you leave town). The only combination café/studio in Quebec, consider it if you're looking for something unique when traveling with children.

SECRET
CULTURE

❧

During a visit in 1981, German film director Rainer Werner Fassbinder expressed his exuberance about the city's cultural offerings: "Montreal seems to me the highest point of hope for culture in the western world."

There are several **Maisons de la Culture** (Cultural Centers) around the city, which often play host to special exhibits. One of these, the *Maison de la Culture Maisonneuve* (4120 Ontario East, tel: 872-2200), is housed at the old market building.

Other maisons are listed below:

- **Ahuntsic** (12137 Bois de Boulogne, tel: 872-8749)

- **Centre d'Histoire de Montréal** (335 Place d'Youville, tel: 872-3207)

- **Chapelle Historique du Bon Pasteur** (100 Sherbrooke East, tel: 872-5338)
- **Côte des Neiges** (5920 Côte des Neiges, tel: 872-6889)
- **La Petite Patrie** (6707 de Lorimier, tel: 872-1730)
- **Marie Uguay** (6052 Monk, tel: 872-2044)
- **Mercier** (8105 Hochelaga, tel: 872-8755)
- **Notre Dame de Grâce** (3755 Botrel, tel: 872-2157)
- **Parc Frontenac** (2550 Ontario East, tel: 872-7882)
- **Plateau Mont Royal** (465 Mont Royal East, tel: 872-2266)
- **Pointe aux Trembles** (8075 Hochelaga, Pointe aux Trembles, tel: 872-2240)
- **Rivière des Prairies** (9140 Perras, Rivière des Prairies, tel: 872-9814)
- **Villeray St. Michel Parc Extension** (7920 St. Laurent, tel: 872-6131)

Exhibits change regularly, so phone ahead to find out what's going on at any given time. Among the shows recently presented were a history of the cultivation, marketing, and social impact of tea in various countries, a history of children's fables for adults, and art from the Caribbean.

SECRET
CYCLING

✤

Maison des Cyclistes (1251 Rachel East, just west of Papineau, across from *Parc Lafontaine*, tel: 521-8356) is the home of Vélo Québec (Quebec Cycling) and the official meeting place for cycling enthusiasts. All the information you will ever need about cycling in the city and around the province can be found here, including detailed maps of bike paths thoughout the region. And even if you aren't looking for anything in particular, stop in at their **Café Bicycletta** for a cappuccino break amongst like-minded pedalers.

Though not systematically interconnected, the island does have several bike paths and bicycle reserved lanes. Following are a few of the routes worth exploring.

The bicycle path from *Old Montreal* to the **Lachine Canal** is perhaps the most scenic and interesting for visitors. This trail resonates with the history of the fur trade and the struggle waged by early inhabitants against the barrier that was the Lachine Rapids. Begin at the Old Port, where Parks Canada maintains the **Maison des Éclusiers** (corner of McGill and de la Commune), an interpretation center dedicated to the history of the construction of the canal, the first instrument of navigation allowing for penetration from the St. Lawrence into the Great Lakes system. Just outside the Maison are the first locks of the canal system.

The path wends its way along the canal for 11 km, passing by *Marché Atwater*, all the way to Lachine, where you'll find the **Monk Pavilion** (711 St. Joseph, corner of 7th Avenue, Lachine), another

Parks Canada interpretation center. Both centers are open daily from mid-May until Labor Day (for information on the Lachine Canal historic site, contact Parks Canada at 283-6054 or 637-7433). Also at the Lachine end of the canal is the **Fur Trade National Historic Site** (1255 St. Joseph, tel: 637-7433), featuring the only remaining warehouse from the 19th-century fur trade, and an interactive museum that brings the fur-trading era to life.

Boulevard Gouin runs pretty much the entire length of the north end of the island. Much of it has reserved bike lanes, running parallel to the Rivière des Prairies. Gouin also passes three of the *Nature Parks* (*Cap St. Jacques*, *Bois de Liesse*, and *Pointe aux Prairies*).

In the area of town known as ***Plateau Mont Royal***, which lies just east of the mountain, dedicated cycling lanes can be found along Rachel (running east and west) and Brébeuf (running north and south). The paths connect at beautiful *Parc Lafontaine*. Every Tuesday evening through June and July, you can explore the plateau on a guided cycling tour (tel: 521-8356).

The city is quite welcoming to cyclists, notwithstanding the reputation local drivers enjoy for being aggressive. Evidence of this is in the annual **Tour de l'Île** (tel: 521-8356), the world's largest bicycle rally, which monopolizes city streets for a day in early June. In an attempt to keep the event manageable, organizers strictly limit the number of participants. If you intend to be in Montreal when the tour is on, contact the organizers as early as possible to obtain an entry form.

SECRET
DELIS

Schwartz's Montreal Hebrew Delicatessen (3895 St. Laurent, tel: 842-4813) is nothing short of a landmark. Virtually everyone who ventures off Montreal's most well-beaten tracks has eaten here, but we've included this smoked-meat haven in the guide because you *don't* want to miss it. It's one of the reasons Montreal-style smoked meat is celebrated far and wide. Abandon your low-fat diet for a day and enjoy.

Literally across the street from Schwartz's — it's a coin toss where you should eat — is the **Main St. Lawrence Steak House Delicatessen** (3864 St. Laurent, tel: 843-8126). The Main offers you more elbow room — it's actually got booths — so you don't have to share the salt with strangers. And you gotta love a place that still refers to St. Laurent as St. Lawrence.

Ben's (990 de Maisonneuve West, corner of Metcalfe, tel: 844-1000; Metro: Peel) is another smoked-meat landmark, though its allure has faded since its heyday. The walls are lined with autographed photos of celebrities from the 1950s and 1960s that anyone under the age of 50 is defied to recognize.

Though the word *institution*, like *legend*, is way overused, both apply to **Wilensky's** (34 Fairmount West, corner of St. Urbain, tel: 271-0247). No Montreal Jew hasn't eaten at this 70-year-old lunch counter, and most Montrealers, regardless of ethnic origin, know of the place. It was given wide exposure as a prominent set in the film version of Mordecai Richler's *The Apprenticeship of Duddy Kravitz*. However, unlike in the movie, there are no tables and chairs, just a half-dozen stools at the counter. No need to consider the menu, just order the special.

Euro-Deli (3619 St. Laurent, north of des Pins, tel: 843-7853) is a trendy choice among the university crowd.

SECRET

DINERS

The aluminum **Galaxie Diner** (4801 St. Denis, at Gilford, tel: 499-9711), shaped like an old railcar, looks like it rocked into town straight off the set of *American Graffiti*. In fact, it was moved to Montreal as a pre-fab from Boston. It serves healthy portions of traditional diner fare. Try it for a hearty breakfast. As you look out on Gilford, know that you're seeing one of the few major streets in the city that run diagonally.

A genuine Montreal original, **Orange Julep** (7700 Décarie, corner of Paré, tel: 738-7486; if you're on the Décarie Expressway, get off at the Jean Talon exit; Metro: Namur) is as recognizable as the mountain. You can't miss the humongous orange-shaped and -colored monstrosity that serves up the frothiest, most thirst-quenching orange beverage — the orange julep — ever put in a glass on a hot summer day. Don't be shy about digging into the steamed hot dogs and greasy fries, either. The Julep is one of the last genuine drive-ins left. There's no dining area, just a counter and a parking lot, so enjoy eating in the comfort of your own vehicle. Whenever the heat gets to you is a good time for a julep, but make your visit on a Wednesday night between 19:00 and 22:00, when vintage cars gather to further enhance the '50s feel. The Julep is only open during the summer.

Those in the know say that eating at **Restaurant Chez Clo** (3199 Ontario East, corner of Dézéry in *Hochelaga-Maisonneuve*, tel: 522-5348), an inexpensive, very authentic neighborhood French Canadian eatery, is like eating at their mom's.

Magnan (2602 St. Patrick, tel: 935-9647; take Charlevoix from Notre Dame West to cross the canal; Metro: Charlevoix) is an authentic tavern in the old style, except that women are now welcome (in the old days, taverns were male-only retreats). Magnan can reasonably claim the best hamburger steak in the city. They smother it, and any other beef you want, with an incomparable, thick pepper sauce. With sports on big screens and beer by the pitcher, closing time is the only excuse for leaving. Set aside Monday at lunch for a visit and witness the live broadcast of Gilles Proulx's call-in radio show on CKAC between 11:30 and 14:00. This firebrand nationalist is one of the biggest media stars in the city. His broadcasts are in French.

SECRET
ENVIRONMENT

The **Biodôme** (4777 Pierre de Coubertin, between Pie IX and Viau, tel: 868-3000; Metro: Viau) contains a fascinating recreation of four distinct ecosystems, replete with plant life and small animals. Because there are no oversized creatures penned in under-sized enclosures, this is one zoo-like attraction that won't break an animal lover's heart. The animals all have plenty of space within their habitats, and — as you'll experience upon entering the steamy tropical section, in particular — the Biodôme is designed and maintained for the comfort of its inhabitants, not the visitors. A couple of times a year, it opens at night to allow a glimpse into the nocturnal world (call ahead to find out when). Open daily 09:00 to 18:00, until 20:00 in the summer. Admission is $8.50 for adults. ⓯

America's landmark pavilion for Expo '67, a huge geodesic dome designed by Buckminster Fuller, has been transformed into the **Biosphere** (160 Chemin Tour de l'Île, *Île Ste. Hélène*, tel: 283-5000; Metro: Île Ste. Hélène), an interactive museum dedicated to sen-sitizing visitors to the fragility of one of our most overlooked precious resources: water. The focus is on the St. Lawrence–Great Lakes ecosystem. The island location has an added bonus: this vantage point gives you one of the most spectacular views of the city. Adults $6.50, seniors and students $5, children $4. ⓰

Ecomuseum (21125 Chemin Ste. Marie, *Ste. Anne de Bellevue*, tel: 457-9449; take Highway 40 [TransCanada] west from Montreal to exit 41 and follow the signs to Chemin Ste. Marie) gives you the opportunity to view wolves, bears, lynx, foxes, raccoons, porcupines, deer, bald eagles, owls, and other species native to the St. Lawrence Valley over the course of a walk through a beautiful park, including a marshland. Open daily 09:00 to 17:00. Adults $4, seniors $3, children 5 to 12 $2. ⓱

Boasting 25 km of meandering wooded trails, the **Morgan Arboretum** (Chemin Ste. Marie, *Ste. Anne de Bellevue*, tel: 398-7812; you'll pass it just before you reach the *Ecomuseum*) is the largest arboretum in Canada. If you're around in late March or early April, call to arrange a visit to the *cabane à sucre* (sugar shack), a Quebec tradition to mark the collection of maple syrup. The arboretum has the oldest cabane on the island. Definitely an attraction with year-round appeal, the *Morgan Arboretum* is a particular treat in the fall when the leaves spectacularly change color. ⓱

SECRET
ESPIONAGE

In July 1996, a most interesting guidebook went on sale in Moscow. KGB *Guidebook to Cities of the World* offers insight into where and how Russian KGB agents carried on in Paris, London, Rome, New York, Bangkok, Cairo, and Mexico City. It describes their favorite routes for foiling surveillance, restaurants and parks where they met with informants, and the places where milestones in Cold War espionage happened. Unfortunately, Montreal is nowhere to be found in this volume.

Despite the KGB's apparent lack of activity in this city, Montreal has nonetheless been a backdrop for intrigue over the years. In particular, during the American Civil War, Montreal was a hotbed of secret activity. The now disappeared **St. Lawrence Hall**, which once stood at the corner of St. Jacques and St. François-Xavier in *Old Montreal*, was the hotel where both the Confederate spy chief and a contingent of the British army were lodged for a time. Here, Southern spies conspired to rob a bank at St. Alban's, Vermont, to finance the war effort. The plot was uncovered, and they were tried at the old *Palais de Justice*. The conspirators ended up staying in Montreal.

St. Lawrence Hall also housed John Wilkes Booth during a visit to the city. It is rumored that he spent part of his time in Montreal planning Abraham Lincoln's assassination.

Following the Civil War, Confederate leader Jefferson Davis sought respite in Montreal. He penned part of his autobiography here, while staying in a house on the east side of de la Montagne, south of Ste. Catherine. Where the house once stood is now a parking lot, but it was situated right next to 1181 de la Montagne (now the headquarters of *Heritage Montreal*) and was identical to that residence. A plaque commemorating Davis's sojourn is mounted on the Bay storefront on Ste. Catherine West and Union.

Montreal was no Berlin or Geneva, but like far more obscure places, it was nevertheless touched by the Cold War. In the old days, if you loitered for too long outside the **Soviet Consulate** (3655 du Musée, north of Docteur Penfield), a true-to-life Communist functionary would come out to demand your business. Things may have lightened up since the Russian Federation took over the property, but maybe not. Linger or take photographs of the stately mansion to find out. Even more imposing is the fortress built into the side of the mountain at the northeast corner of Cedar and des Pins. This is the **Cuban Consulate** (1415 des Pins West), reputedly the nerve center for Cuban espionage directed against North America. Security cameras scour the perimeter for subversives. No one really knows what goes on in there — even when it caught fire several years back, machine-gun toting diplomats kept fire-fighters at bay while two of their colleagues died in the blaze.

S E C R E T
EXOTICA

Montreal doesn't have a red-light district so much as a green light to all sorts of exotic entertainment. A stroll through the center of town (along Ste. Catherine, for example) exposes a plethora of strip bars, many of which offer free buffet lunches as added enticement. Our clubs have always been popular with visitors because in Montreal, unlike so many jurisdictions, the strippers are permitted (encouraged, required) to take it *all* off. For an added charge (usually around $6), they'll do it from a stool at your very table (the infamous *danse à table*). Listed below are several establishments that are out of the ordinary.

Brasserie 4040 (4040 Jean Talon, just west of Pie IX) has *serveuses sexy* dishing out the $1.99 breakfasts. For a time, it was quite a fad for brasseries to deck their waitresses out in lingerie or bikinis for the morning rush. The moment seems to have passed, although a few places, including Brasserie 4040, still follow the practice. So, if you like your eggs with a little titillation, breakfast starts at 08:00.

If table dancing just doesn't cut it for you, some strip clubs offer the notorious *danse à dix* — for $10 per song, a girl will strip right in front of you and permit what is euphemistically referred to as *contact*. How much contact, however, is the subject of some controversy. Many of the more established clubs won't permit this activity, but **Solid Gold** (8820 St. Laurent, north of Métropolitain) is one of the nicer clubs to allow it.

Contrary to popular belief, exotic entertainment isn't just for men. Women may want to drop in at **Club 281** (281 Ste. Catherine East, just east of St. Laurent) to watch the men gyrate. Nor is it just for heteros. See *Secret Gay Village*.

Need a haircut? Perhaps just a trim? Unhappy with your current stylist? You'd probably be less inclined to complain about the cut if the girl doing the cutting were at some stage of undress. **Salon Adorable Sexy** (1959 Jean Talon East, east of Papineau, tel: 728-8506; Metro: Fabre) offers hair care with a little extra. For a supplemental charge, the stylists will do their thing while revealing their things.

Fetish Café (1426 Beaudry, north of Ste. Catherine East, tel: 523-3013; Metro: Beaudry) caters to the leather-and-latex set. This isn't the place for gawking — the patrons won't appreciate it — but if you're willing to get into the spirit, this is quite a unique club.

SECRET

FARMS

The **Experimental Farm of MacDonald College** (21111 Bord du Lac, *Ste. Anne de Bellevue*, tel: 398-7701) has cows, chickens, and other barnyard beasts — you know, the whole Old MacDonald thing. Fun for the kids. Open 14:00 to 17:00 8 May to 18 August. Free admission. **⑰**

Ferme l'Autruche Dorée (514 Chemin du Ruisseau Saint-Louis West, Sainte Marie de Monnoir, *Montérégie*, tel: 514-460-4997) provides a rare opportunity to visit an ostrich farm. These comical creatures are gaining popularity as a food source. **⑱**

Boasting 150 animals, **Ferme à Tire d'Ailes** (99 Rang Saint Marie West, Saint Timothée, *Montérégie*, tel: 514-377-6670) offers farm tours. **⑱**

Marie Roselaine (188 St. François, Sherrington, *Montérégie*, tel: 514-454-3659) is a working goat farm that offers tours to visitors. **⑱**

SECRET

FOOTBALL

In 1996 the Baltimore Stallions Canadian Football League fran-chise relocated to Montreal as the reincarnation of the **Alouettes** (tel: 252-4668). The team got off to a rocky start, both on the field and in the stands. They will play at *Olympic Stadium* from late June until November (Pie IX at Sherbrooke; Metro: Pie IX).

Perhaps more spirited is the local university football scene. The **McGill Redmen** (for info, call 398-7003), who play at **Molson Stadium** (des Pins West, just east of University), are credited with introducing a new form of rugby football in 1870, which would develop into the modern Canadian and American games. In 1874 they participated in the first ever intercollegiate football game, against Harvard at Cambridge. Sit in the less comfortable north stands — no seat backs have been installed over the concrete bleachers because this is the side where visiting fans traditionally congregate — for a spectacular fall view of downtown Montreal while you watch the game. ⓘ

Concordia also boasts the football Stingers, playing at **Concordia Stadium at Loyola Campus**. If you don't want to pay for a ticket, just lean on the fence that runs along Sherbrooke Street; if you do, call 848-3862 (on Sherbrooke, at the far-west end, west of Cavendish).

SECRET
FRUITS AND VEGETABLES

Montreal has four open markets, each one brimming with fresh produce of the season, maple syrup, and cut flowers, as well as all the delights carried by the specialty food shops. All four markets are lively and crowded, especially on weekends. **Marché Jean Talon** (immediately south of Jean Talon East at Casgrain, two blocks east of St. Laurent), at the core of *Little Italy*, and **Marché Atwater** (at the southern extremity of Atwater, conveniently located above the *Lachine Canal* bike path) are both open all year (Metro: Lionel Groulx). The Atwater market turns into a veritable forest around Christmas time as tree farmers take up all the exterior space to sell their special crop. **20**

The beautiful beaux-arts centerpiece of the **Marché Maisonneuve** (4120 Ontario East; Metro: Pie IX), built in 1914, is now the area's *Maison de la Culture*, while the outdoor park area is utilized by the market. **13**

Marché St. Jacques, the smallest of the outdoor markets, is located at the corner of Ontario and Amherst, across from the *Musée du Fier Monde* (Metro: Beaudry). **21**

If you like someone else to do the shopping and cooking, try **Pushap** (5195 Paré, just east of Décarie, tel: 737-4527; Metro: Namur; and 11999 Gouin West, Pierrefonds, west of des Sources,

tel: 683-0556) for vegetarian Indian cuisine, or **Manbo Restaurant** (81 de la Gauchetière West, *Chinatown*), a vegetarian Chinese restaurant, where even the sign outside boasts that the cuisine is healthy.

Le Commensal (2115 St. Denis; 1204 McGill College; 3715 Queen Mary, across from *St. Joseph's Oratory*) offers imaginative and extensive dining. The best thing about this restaurant (at least for meat lovers) is the variety of dishes that don't taste vegetarian. The chefs work wonders with tofu and seitan. The food is served buffet-style, but while you're heaping food on your plate, keep in mind that you pay by weight.

Two regions, the *Laurentides* to the north of Montreal (take Highway 15, the Autoroute des Laurentides, from Montreal) and the *Monterégie* to the south (take the Champlain Bridge to Highway 10), offer opportunities to experience agrotourism. *Apple picking* is a very popular activity. The season runs roughly from August into October.

Montérégie apple orchards are concentrated in Mont Saint Grégoire, Mont Saint Hillaire, and Rougemont. Alternatively, you can go strawberry picking in Saint Hubert, Saint Jean sur Richelieu, and Salaberry de Valleyfield. The area is also renowned for its vineyards — in Havelock, Iberville, Napierville, Sabrevois, and Saint Bernard de Lacolle — and cideries — in Hemmingford, Mont Saint Grégoire, Mont Saint Hillaire, and Rougemont. Check with the local tourist office before going to verify what's in season and where you'll find the best crops at any particular time (call for tourist information Monday to Friday 09:00 to 17:00, 514-674-5555). ⑱

In the **Laurentides**, apples, pears, corn, plums, pumpkins, strawberries, and raspberries can all be found, depending on the season, in Blainville, *Oka*, Saint Joseph du Lac, or Sainte Anne des Plaines. Call ahead to verify the availability of the produce and for recommendations on the best orchards (call for tourist information daily 09:00 to 17:00, 514-436-8532 or 800-561-6673).

S E C R E T

GALLERIES

❧

Because the gallery exhibits are constantly changing, your best bet is to consult the listings mentioned under "Other Resources" at the time of your visit. The galleries listed below have a reputation for particularly interesting shows.

Galerie d'Art de Bougainville (4511 St. Denis, tel: 845-2400)

Galerie Christiane Chassay (tel: 875-0071), **B-312 Émergence** (tel: 874-9423), **Circa** (tel: 393-8248), **Espace 414** (tel: 274-3447), **Galerie 524** (tel: 270-1578), **Lieu Ouest** (tel: 393-7255), **Observatoire 4** (tel: 866-5320), **René Blouin** (tel: 393-9969), and **Galerie Trois Points** (tel: 866-8008) are all located in a nondescript office tower at 372 Ste. Catherine West. You'd drive right by it, never suspecting it houses such a wealth of art, unless you knew to look for it.

Galerie Eric Devlin (tel: 866-6272), **Conseil de la Sculpture** (tel: 879-1962), **Conseil de la Peinture** (tel: 876-3632), **Dare-**

Dare (tel: 844-8327), and **Occurrence** (tel: 397-0236) are all to be found just a few doors down from the above in another office building, at 460 Ste. Catherine West.

Galerie de l'UQAM (Université du Québec à Montréal, 1400 Berri, Room J-R120, tel: 987-8421; Metro: Berri-UQAM).

Leonard & Bina Ellen Art Gallery (Concordia University, 1400 de Maisonneuve West, tel: 848-4750; Metro: Guy-Concordia) emphasizes Canadian artists.

Galerie Pink (1456 Notre Dame West, tel: 935-9851; Metro: Lionel Groulx) emphasizes the avant-garde.

S E C R E T
GARDENS

⚜

The **Botanical Gardens** (main entrance at the corner of Pie IX and Sherbrooke East, tel: 872-1400; Metro: Pie IX) is hardly a hidden treasure, but some of its attractions and special events are. A brand new feature that just opened in 1996 is the House of Trees, situated at the northern edge of the gardens, off Rosemont Boulevard. This permanent exhibit explains the importance of trees the world over. Open 09:00 to 18:00 year round, until 20:00 from 22 June to 2 September. Adults $8.75, seniors $6.50, children $4.50.

Among the special events held annually at the gardens, my personal favorite is the captivating **Chinese Lanterns** (La Magie des Lanternes), which are lit every evening until closing at 21:00 from the end of September through October. These artistic marvels cast magic around the Chinese gardens.

Montrealers are always looking for some way to make the best of our frigid winters, especially come February, when the good cheer of Christmas is all but forgotten and the thaw of April is so terribly far away. The annual creation of ice sculptures, on display in the gardens every February, succeeds in taking advantage of the weather to make something wonderful.

My least favorite activity is the **annual bug tasting**, hosted by the Insectarium. Yes, this paragraph was proofread several times — this is no misprint. Every February, you can wreak your revenge on the little creatures who, during the summer months, invade your home, chomp on your flesh, and spoil your picnics. For dessert: butterfly-larvae lollipops. I can't comment with any authority on the event, since I never have and never will sample the goods. No publisher will ever pay me enough to change this policy.

In 1980 Montreal hosted the wildly successful international floral festival. Its legacy survives on *Île Ste. Hélène* in **Les Floralies** (take the Jacques Cartier Bridge to the Parc des Îles exit and follow the signs; Metro: Île Ste. Hélène). Consisting of 19 different gardens, this is a lovely place for a stroll in the company of flowers and water. **16**

SECRET

GAY VILLAGE

Montreal's Gay Village itself is not at all hidden. It's a lively and popular nightlife district where the gay community congregates, and where straights often go to experience the restaurants and a number of the dance clubs. Keep in mind that some of the bars are gay only. The spine of the Village is Ste. Catherine East, between Berri and Papineau (Metro: Berri-UQAM or Beaudry).

Piccolo Diavolo (1336 Ste. Catherine East, tel: 526-1336) is a charming Italian restaurant with rich decor and a very interesting menu. Highly recommended to all.

Le Saloon (1333 Ste. Catherine East, tel: 522-1333) is the brainchild of the same people who own Diavolo. It offers a varied menu, from Thai to Mexican, with a focus on healthy cuisine. Upstairs is **Le Lounge du Saloon**, a relaxing club with live entertainment — usually jazz — Thursday through Sunday. On the last Wednesday of every month, Le Lounge hosts a live drag show (there's an entrance fee for this event).

Cabaret L'Entre Peau (1115 Ste. Catherine East, tel: 525-7566) features shows by female impersonators.

Bar Stock (1278 St. André, south of Ste. Catherine, tel: 842-1336) is an off-the-beaten-path male strip club for men.

Sisters (1456 Ste. Catherine East, tel: 522-8357) is a popular lesbian club located in the **Home** complex, which houses several gay nightspots.

Groove Society (1008 Ste. Catherine East, tel: 284-1999) is a dance club that welcomes both gays and straights.

SECRET
GLASS

Glass is a much overlooked artistic medium. At **Galerie Elena Lee** (1428 Sherbrooke West, tel: 844-6009, in the midst of Sherbrooke's row of exclusive art and antique dealers; Metro: Guy-Concordia), which staged a 20th anniversary exhibition in the fall of 1996, glass receives its due. The gallery, which could easily be mistaken for a museum, is dedicated to showcasing the finest glassblowing artists. The graceful, sensuous pieces almost beg to be fondled. Souvenir hunters can choose from the exquisite — and reasonably priced — selection of glass perfume bottles, goblets, and candlesticks.

Espace Verre (1200 Mill, just before the Victoria Bridge, tel: 933-6849) has periodic exhibits. This is the workshop for many glassblowers, so it offers a good opportunity to watch the craftsmen at work, as well as a place to view their wares.

SECRET

GOLF

Few golf courses remain within Montreal itself. If you ever desire to have your good walk spoiled, however, there is a hidden nine-hole par three at what was the **Olympic Village** complex (on Viau at Sherbrooke, right across from the *Botanical Gardens*, one block east of the *Olympic Stadium*; Metro: Viau).

If you want to refine your stroke without the frustrations and potential embarrassments of chasing after stray golf balls on a playing course, there are two driving ranges available for endless practice: **Golf Gardens** (7745 Côte de Liesse, off the Décarie Circle toward Dorval Airport, tel: 341-4801), and **Golf de Pratique Île des Soeurs** (on Boulevard Île des Soeurs, immediately after you get onto the island from University, tel: 761-5900). The latter, located just five minutes south of downtown, offers a beautiful suburban setting in which to while away the time smacking golf balls.

SECRET

GREEK

The original **Arahova Souvlaki** (254 St. Viateur West, east of du Parc, tel: 274-7828), now a chain of three, is located in the Greek section of town. Divided into two parts — the souvlaki fast-food side, and the slightly more decorative full-menu side — this is the place for a quick bite or a sit-down dinner that'll leave you feeling full for hours.

Nowhere will you get a plate with more food piled on than at the **Amazona Restaurant** (5525 Côte St. Luc, just west of Décarie, at the corner of Girouard, tel: 484-2612). Main dishes are accompanied, not by a choice of salad, rice, or potato, but by all three. Make this your meal for the day, or maybe the week.

Restaurant Hermes (1010 Jean Talon West, west of du Parc, tel: 272-3880) offers authentic Greek cuisine, including all the classic dishes, homemade in the traditional manner. It's like eating in your mother's dining room. As seems to be a requirement in Greek restaurants, the portions are overly generous.

SECRET
HIGH TECH

Are you one of those people who gets antsy when denied access to your e-mail? Do you fear travel because it'll tear you away from your favorite chat group? Do you feel as though the world's passing you by if you don't get in your regular dose of Net surfing? Luckily for you, several coffee houses catering to the wired crowd can be found around town.

Café Électronique (405 St. Sulpice, corner of St. Paul, tel: 849-1612; Metro: Place d'Armes), the dean of the cyber-set, is in *Old Montreal*.

CyberMind (1718 Ste. Catherine West, east of McGill College, tel: 396-7878; Metro: McGill) is right downtown.

Café Inter Net Central (1431 Bishop, above Ste. Catherine, tel: 288-1638; Metro: Guy-Concordia) is also in the western part of the city's core.

CyberParc (5316 du Parc, tel: 273-7272) is in *Outremont*.

Cyber Bistro (350 Notre Dame West, corner of St. Pierre, tel: 281-6777; Metro: Place d'Armes) also provides Internet access in *Old Montreal*.

Web Site Café (60 Ste. Anne, *Ste. Anne de Bellevue*, tel: 457-1661) is on the West Island.

All offer Internet connections, but none are cheap. Expect to pay in the neighborhood of $5 to plug in for half an hour. CyberMind also offers a wide range of CD-ROMS, video games, interactive competitive gaming, and virtual-reality adventures. All serve coffee and meals.

For those who prefer virtuality to reality, try the interactive adventure of **Laser Quest** (1226 Ste. Catherine West, tel: 393-3000; Metro: Peel). Open Monday to Thursday 17:00 to 23:00, Saturday 12:00 to 01:00, and Sunday 12:00 to 23:00.

Bar Bacci (3553 St. Laurent, just below Prince Arthur, tel: 287-9331) offers a selection of interactive computer games while you drink. They also have pool tables, so you can partake of the original interactive bar sport.

SECRET
HISTORY

Much of Montreal's early history is conspicuously *not* hidden, concentrated as it is in *Old Montreal* and near the Old Port, prime tourist meccas. However, due to a succession of fires that ravaged the city in the 1600s and 1700s and the construction schemes launched prior to the 1970s, before the conservation of landmark sites became fashionable, much of Montreal's past has disappeared. In this brief look at historic Montreal, the object is to give you reason to look at the city differently and to explore in a different direction from the pack.

Though certainly an infant by Old World standards, Montreal is one of the oldest cities in North America. The nineteenth of May 1535 is the date that Jacques Cartier, on his second voyage from St. Malo, pierced the wedge of the Gulf of St. Lawrence and entered the river itself, navigating all the way to the island of Montreal. It is generally accepted that his landing site was Pointe à Callière, which is where Samuel de Champlain would establish the settlement of Place Royale in 1611.

Pointe à Callière is today marked by the distinctive and purposefully modern clock tower of the **Museum of Archaeology and History** (350 Place Royale, corner of de la Commune, tel: 872-9150; Metro: Place d'Armes). The museum stands over the archaeological crypt of the city's first Catholic cemetery. During September, the museum offers guided walking tours of archaeological sites and digs in the Old Montreal area (Wednesdays from

12:00 to 14:00, weekends from 14:00 to 16:00). The museum proper is open all year round (call for times and prices). **24**

From his landing site, Cartier visited the Iroquois settlement of Hochelaga, a formidable community of about 3,500 people living in 50 houses surrounded by a wooden palisade. We'll come back to Hochelaga soon enough. Cartier also climbed to the summit of *Mount Royal*, more of a challenge in the 1500s than the pleasant stroll it entails today.

There was no permanent French settlement between the time of Champlain and the foundation of the mission city of Ville Marie by the Sieur de Maisonneuve, who also landed at Pointe à Callière, in 1642 (while the actual settlements have been known by different names, the island has always been called Montreal).

In 1672, Bénigne Basset was placed in charge of laying out Montreal's first streets. **Rue St. Paul**, a cobblestone thoroughfare that today can barely accommodate two lanes of cars and sidewalks for pedestrians, was the original main street. The northern extremity was **Rue Notre Dame**, upon which would be built the *Notre Dame Cathedral*. The western extremity was at **Rue St. Pierre**, the eastern at **Bonsecours**, where you can now see the resplendent dome of the old **Marché Bonsecours**. **25**

The various north-south cross-streets in between were laid out gradually. **Rue St. Jacques** — which is the heart of today's financial district, and was for decades the financial center of Canada — was set out in 1678, marking a major extension beyond Notre Dame.

Walk the old city with a mind to the past, to the wilderness and dangers that threatened to overwhelm the first French inhabitants of the island. For a good 20 years after Ville Marie was established, there were intermittent clashes with the Iroquois who lived in the

forests beyond. Because of the menace posed by the Iroquois, Maisonneuve was compelled to confine settlers to the fort.

On 6 January 1643, de Maisonneuve made an exception. Leaving the fort, he carried a heavy wooden cross along a path that had been cleared to the summit of *Mount Royal*, where the cross was erected as a gesture of thanks to God for His intercession the previous month in holding back the flooding St. Pierre River, which had threatened to inundate the settlement. (This procession is commemorated in one of the stained glass windows at *Notre Dame Cathedral*.) In 1924 the St. Jean Baptiste Society donated the illuminated cross that presently stands at the peak of *Mount Royal*. It is lit nightly, a beacon to the Christian piety boasted by the New French.

The Sulpician Seminary (116 Notre Dame West) of 1683 is the oldest building still occupied to this day by descendants of its original inhabitants. A plaque stands at the site of the original seminary, built in 1661 at Frothinghan and Workman Court, off *St. Paul.* 🉑

In 1722, engineer Gaspard-Joseph Chaussegros de Léry was commissioned to build fortifications to protect Montreal against feared English incursions. By this time, peace with the Iroquois had been in effect for some two decades and land was being occupied by French settlers well beyond the city limits. The 5.5-metre-high stone fortifications, complete with 13 bastions and cannons, enclosed the area that roughly corresponds to today's **Old Montreal** district: from **de la Commune** at the south, north to **St. Antoine**, and from **Berri** in the east to **McGill** in the west. No attacks were ever launched against these battlements, and they were torn down in the early 19th century.

The absolute best time to explore Old Montreal is early in the morning, before the crush of cars, tourists, and workers drown out the haunting echoes of those first Montrealers. Walk the cobblestone to the sound of your own footsteps and imagine the padding natives just beyond this foreign encroachment. Try to ignore the modern downtown edifices and thoroughfares that now engulf the historic center and picture instead a lush wilderness. Begin your own explorations with inspiration from those who braved the unknown to plant the seeds of all that modernity now surrounding you. (If your imagination needs help, Brian Moore's novel *Black Robe*, which has been adapted as a film, is highly recommended.)

From the old city, follow McGill north to where it becomes **Beaver Hall Hill**. It is here that the fur-trade industry established its headquarters, and from whence the trappers headed out into the wilderness of the interior, past the daunting rapids of Lachine. Climb Beaver Hall Hill and find yourself in the heart of downtown Montreal.

Go as far north as Sherbrooke, then west until you reach the campus of *McGill University*. Pass through the Roddick Gates, and turn to your left, where you will find the **Hochelaga Memorial Stone**, dedicated in 1925. It marks the spot where the best historical guess places the original site of the Hochelaga settlement visited by Cartier. As the settlement was abandoned without a trace before Champlain's arrival, however, no one can be absolutely sure that the marking is accurate. **㉗**

Those up for the strenuous leg of the tour can venture from here to *Mount Royal*, at whose foot the campus rests. Peeking out from behind a skyscraper-pierced cityscape, the mountain appears to be far less dominant than it would have been for Cartier or de

Maisonneuve. But there was a time when it was not so tamely landscaped. ❷❽

From *McGill*, you can go west a couple of blocks to Peel Street, and trek up to where it meets *Mount Royal* at des Pins. Here you will confront the Snake Path, a winding, paved trail that meets up with the main path ringing the mountain. Head west and you'll be transported up to the nature-interpretation center, the chalet, and the lookout, and eventually the cross (not to be confused with the CBC/*Radio Canada* transmission tower, which you will also encounter).

Needless to say, this is not the most convenient way to see Montreal. For most people, the walk from *Old Montreal* to the summit of *Mount Royal* is too long and strenuous. You may prefer to drive or take the Metro from the old city to *McGill*. If you decide to spend a day in this fashion, you should definitely revisit *Old Montreal* and downtown to see the sights you skipped in exchange for covering a wide swath of territory. The point of the route described here is not to cram as many tourist monuments in as quickly as possible, but to experience Montreal from a different perspective, to relive its history in a personal way, to recognize what it was in the 17th century in contrast to what it is today.

SECRET
HOCKEY

Montreal's true sports shrine, its temple, its Valhalla, its *monument nationale* is — or was — the **Forum**. Built in 1924 and renovated several times afterward, the Forum finally hosted its last **Canadiens** game on 11 March 1996 (for trivia buffs, the hometown Habs beat the Dallas Stars). The building still stands squat and muscular at the corner of Ste. Catherine and Atwater (Metro: Atwater), but one fears that it will soon take on a derelict air unless the city quickly decides what to do with it. Hockey fans are still invited to pass by and pay homage. Do so on a winter Saturday night, when it will undoubtedly be loneliest, and listen to the echoes of Richard, Beliveau, Lafleur, Dryden, Robinson, et al. The tears shed during the closing ceremonies last year were genuine. Few Montrealers are without their memories of this magnificent place. **㉙**

The Habs' new digs are the **Molson Centre** (de la Montagne and de la Gauchetière; Metro: Place Bonaventure), where they opened on 16 March against the New York Rangers (and won). Cleaner, newer, and therefore with less color and character, the arena's wider, padded seats in the reds (the most expensive) mean that your thighs won't chafe against your neighbor the whole game and you'll actually be able to remove your bulky overcoat and feel like you've taken it off. But the critics who raved about the new building never ventured up to the cheap seats (the thin row of whites and blues located about a mile above the ice). You can get severe vertigo from the sheer drop as you look down to ice level, and there aren't any seatbelts, but what are you going to do — progress is progress. ㉚

Canadiens tickets are very hard to come by during the season (for what it's worth, call 932-2584). Nearly every game is sold out. If you're planning your trip in advance, contact the team as soon as possible to place an order. For some of the NHL's lesser lights, the cheaper seats go at a less frantic pace. The other alternative is to deal with the entrepreneurs who sell tickets on game night (you know, scalpers). When the opposition is good, the prices they demand will be accordingly high. But remember, this is a supply-and-demand enterprise. Once the game's over, the product is worth nothing. Best advice: wait until they're singing the national anthem (so many people in Quebec don't stand anyway) and then try to bargain. If the scalpers have anything left, you can start to see the desperation in their eyes. Now's the time to buy. Or to go to **Moe's Deli and Bar** (1050 de la Montagne, tel: 931-6637) right across the street and watch the game up close on a big screen.

Even if you can't get into the Molson Centre for a game or a show, you can take a tour during the off hours (call 989-2765 for details).

Univers Maurice Rocket Richard (2800 Viau, south of Sher-brooke, at the eastern end of the Olympic site, tel: 251-9930; Metro: Viau), located in the Maurice Richard Arena, this museum is dedicated to the life and career of Montreal's most celebrated hockey legend. Memorabilia and photographs pay tribute to Richard, who dominated the NHL during his era and captured the imagination of his hometown fans as few have done since. Admission is free and the museum is open Tuesday through Sunday 12:00 to 18:00.

To go even further back in hockey history, the first game played before the public was on 3 March 1875, at the **Victoria Skating Rink**, whose dimensions were 200 feet by 85 feet, which became the North American standard. That structure, behind the Sheraton Centre Hotel (north of René Lévesque, between Drummond and Stanley), is now a Tilden garage.

A viable hockey alternative is to go down to the **Verdun Auditorium** (4110 Lasalle, in Verdun, tel: 765-7130; Metro: De l'Église) to catch Quebec Major Junior Hockey League action. The Verdun Junior Canadiens play their home games here. Tickets are very reasonably priced and the games are a lot of fun. You can't be anywhere but close to the action. And you'll get to see players who'll be in the NHL in a couple of years' time.

Another outlet for the hockey buff is to watch university hockey action when the **McGill Redmen** play at the **McConnell Winter Stadium** (all the way at the top of University, north of des Pins, tel: 398-7000). **⑲**

The **Concordia Stingers** play at the **Athletic Complex at Loyola Campus** (Sherbrooke, at the far western end, near Cavendish, tel: 848-3862).

SECRET
HORSES

Long before the Casino de Montréal at *Île Notre Dame* gave people the opportunity to fritter away large sums of money on long odds, Blue Bonnets served the same purpose. Established in 1906, the track has been renovated and rechristened the **Hippodrôme de Montréal** (7440 Décarie, at Jean Talon, tel: 739-2741; Metro: Namur), becoming a decidedly more upscale venue in the process.

Visit the **Montreal Police Cavalry** stables on *Mount Royal*, just beyond *Beaver Lake*. The officers on duty will be more than happy to give you a tour and introduce you to their equine partners. The post is open 09:30 to 11:00 and 13:00 to 16:00. You may find the stables unmanned if all officers are on patrol, but usually there is someone present during the posted hours.

SECRET
HOT DOGS

Paris has its steak-frites, Montreal has its steamie-frites. The difference between a dog in Montreal and elsewhere is that the wiener and bun are steamed, rather than grilled. Some places serve both, so specify the steamie.

Nobody's shot pool here in decades, but the **Montreal Pool Room** (1200 St. Laurent, south of Ste. Catherine) serves up the yardstick against which all steamies and fries are judged. No seats, just lean against the bar. Pick a spot nearest the salt and vinegar. At the Pool Room, situated in the heart of Montreal's red-light district on the seamy part of the Main, you're just as likely to dine with the cops as their quarry. Makes for a great cheap meal with ambiance. Nutrition? Well, I'm no expert.

Boulangerie La Rencontre (5201 St. Urbain, smack on the corner of Fairmount) is a small lunch counter that offers what might well be the only Chilean hot dog in town (a Vienna sausage topped with mayo, tomatoes, onions, and mustard), along with a selection of other Chilean sandwiches. Nothing on the menu costs more than $3.25. The presence of a Chilean establishment in the heart of the old Jewish and Greek quarter is testimony to the evolving immigration patterns of Montreal.

Lafleur (central locations include 5383 Notre Dame East, 2120 Ontario East, and 3620 St. Denis) is a classic steamie emporium. Originally one drive-through stand at 475 St. Jacques in Ville St. Pierre, at the junction with Highway 20, Lafleur has expanded into a multi-outlet chain.

La Belle Province (outlets include 1604 Mont Royal East, 3001 Notre Dame West, 1 Ste. Catherine East, 1018 Ste. Catherine East, and 3929 Sherbrooke East) is another home-grown dog chain. Try the Quebec original, poutine: french fries covered in a gloopy gravy over melted cheese curds.

SECRET
HUMOR

Writing about the humor he found during his 1874–75 visit to Montreal, Englishman Samuel Butler commented, "When I was there I found their jokes like their roads — very long, and not very good, leading to little tin points of a spire which has been remorselessly obvious for miles without seeming to get any nearer." Well, much has changed in the intervening century or so since Butler's time, though not everything: Montreal's roads, ravaged by wild temperature fluctuations and the rough treatment of heavy snow-removal equipment and corrosive road salts, are still atrocious. A common joke says that a big BUMP sign should be posted on all roads leading into the city to prepare drivers for the cavernous, axle-busting potholes they'll encounter.

Every year in late July, Montreal becomes a very funny place, when it plays host to the world's largest international comedy festival, **Festival Juste pour Rire/Just for Laughs** (call 845-3155 for details). The 1996 edition ran for 12 days and featured some 550 performers in more than 1,000 shows. Over the years, the festival has boasted such stars as Jerry Seinfeld, Tim Allen, Milton Berle, Jonathan Winters, Drew Carey, Bob Newhart, and John Candy. But don't limit yourself to attending shows starring comedians you've heard of. The great pleasure of the festival lies in the discovery of those unknown performers you'll hear about in the future.

Just for Laughs, which began in 1983 as a two-night show, has blossomed over the years and promises only to get bigger. Festival

CEO Andy Nulman asserts that his goal is to "make Montreal the funniest place on earth for two weeks. I want to overtake the city with a spirit of foolishness."

The festival takes place at several venues. The gala shows are at **Théâtre St. Denis** (1594 St. Denis, tel: 849-4211). While this is the site to catch established TV stars, be forewarned that these performances often lack spontaneity. They are taped for later broadcast and, thus, are timed to the second and frequently tamed for prime time. Much more intimate and exciting are the shows at **Club Soda** (5240 du Parc, north of Laurier, tel: 270-7848), is a genuine nightclub that lends the comedy that necessary smoky, boozy atmosphere (most shows here are restricted to an over-18 audience because of the alcohol, so attend the galas if traveling with children). While touristy to the max, check out the *Old Port* for a free look at many of the acts you'd otherwise be paying for.

One of the happy consequences of the festival is the inspiration it gives to the local comedy scene. Year-round comedy clubs like the **Comedy Nest** (1740 René Lévesque West, west of Guy, tel: 932-6378; Metro: Guy-Concordia) and **ComedyWorks** (1238 Bishop, tel: 398-9661) highlight local acts and succeed in attracting major Canadian and international stars. A ticket to either club usually runs $10. Also, check listings for bigger acts, which often play *Club Soda*.

The **Humour Museum** (2111 St. Laurent, just south of Sherbrooke, tel: 845-4000) is worth a visit for its fittingly hilarious tribute to comedy. **③**

Just around the corner from the museum, at 51 Sherbrooke West, is the mansion housing the Just for Laughs administration. This classically sculpted building used to be the home of prolific photographer William Nottman, whose archives, documenting the city and its growth, are held at the **McCord Museum of Canadian History** (690 Sherbrooke West, tel: 398-7100).

SECRET

IMBIBING

In his 1936 travel book, *Crossroads*, Austin F. Cross described this city as "a 24-hour town, with more life on its main street at four in the morning than most cities have at four in the afternoon. Montreal has a permanent case of whoopee." This observation still holds true 60 years later. Closing time for bars is 03:00, but if you still can't bear to go home, you'll have no problem finding an all-night coffee shop filled with the bleary-eyed and the hungover, or a restaurant for the incurably hungry.

For the opportunity to sample various micro-brews during regular drinking hours, try **Le Cheval Blanc** (809 Ontario East, just off St. Denis, tel: 522-0211; Metro: Berri-UQAM), in the heart of one of Montreal's liveliest nightlife quarters, or **Le Sergent Recruteur** (4650 St. Laurent, tel: 287-1412), which also serves up a tantalizing selection of unique beers.

Fûtenbulle (273 Bernard West, east of du Parc, tel: 276-0473), a comfortable neighborhood bar situated a few blocks east of Bernard's main nightlife scene, has a menu of 120 beers from all over the world. Oh, and good food, too.

Like it shaken or stirred? Got a James Bond fixation? **Jello Bar** (151 Ontario East, tel: 285-2621) can satisfy your need with its 50 or so different types of martinis.

Whisky Café (5800 St. Laurent, corner of Bernard, tel: 278-2646) is the place to experience the elegant luxury of single-malt scotches, where the connoisseur can relax and appreciate the subtleties of each particular blend.

Sample different types of single-malt scotch at **Île Noire** (342 Ontario East, tel: 982-0866). What's a Scottish-style pub doing in this neighborhood? Oh well, it's all part of the confused conglomeration that is our fair city.

A library in a pub? I dreamt about such places when I was a student. The **Madhatter Library/Pub** (1463 Metcalfe, tel: 982-1955) is close enough to McGill to influence exam results. Drop in and find out why Johnny can't read. Pool, pinball, foosball, video, and board games are available, along with cheap beer and food.

Foufounes Électriques (87 Ste. Catherine East, just east of St. Laurent, tel: 844-5539; Metro: Place des Arts) is the city's punk landmark. Live alternative shows, Internet hookups, interesting patrons. Police do frequent walk-throughs to keep an eye on those interesting patrons. Fun for everyone.

Bar St. Laurent (3874 St. Laurent, north of des Pins) has pool tables, Latin-beat music, and a big screen for sports. University students and neighborhood habitués make an eclectic mix. There's a cover charge on busy nights.

Le Boréale (3936 St. Laurent, just a block north of Bar St. Laurent). Home of cheap beer and the university crowd it attracts.

SECRET
INDIAN

Taj Mahal de l'Ouest (5026 Sherbrooke West, just east of Décarie, tel: 482-0076) features cuisine from the north and south of India. Calcutta-trained chef Sadeq Choudhury serves up consistently excellent fare. Try it for dinner, or the very well-priced lunch specials. A particular favorite is the chicken tikka dinner, a succulently tender chicken breast braised in the unique tandoori style.

Golden Curry House (5210 St. Laurent, north of Fairmount, tel: 270-2561) is a good choice for lunch or dinner. Prices are very reasonable.

Those in search of vegetarian delights should see *Pushap* in *Secret Fruits and Vegetables*.

SECRET
ITALIAN

Visit **Restaurant Spaghettata** (399 Laurier West, west of du Parc, tel: 273-9509) for gracious Italian dining, including superb pastas elegantly served, and a varied menu that will appeal to all lovers of Italian food.

La Cucina (5134 St. Laurent, between Laurier and Fairmount, tel: 495-1131) is a bistro-style eatery serving pasta, pizza, and calzone. Conveniently, pastas are available in half portions, so you can mix and match, sampling a variety of flavors.

Da Emma (5486 St. Laurent, north of Fairmount, tel: 273-4097) goes for the home-kitchen style. The menu varies according to what the chef has concocted.

Only last year, you couldn't get into **Rôtisserie Italienne** (1933 Ste. Catherine West, east of the *Forum*, tel: 935-4436) on a night when the Canadiens played a home game. Now that the nearby *Forum* has closed, you don't have to check your hockey schedule before deciding to eat here. Great homemade pastas.

S E C R E T

JAPANESE

The upscale **Soto Restaurant Sushi Bar** (3527 St. Laurent, north of Sherbrooke, tel: 842-1150) is located smack in the middle of the hot St. Laurent nightlife scene. If you're a sushi gourmande, or you've been anxiously awaiting the occasion to get in on the craze, you'll find a complete selection of these delicate morsels, as well as a full menu of other Japanese specialties.

S E C R E T

JAZZ

✧

The **Festival International de Jazz de Montréal** (tel: 871-1881) is perhaps the least hidden annual event in the city. For two weeks (from 26 June to 6 July in 1997) everyone pretends to be a jazz lover, and true afficionados congregate from all over the world. The jazz festival is the locals' harbinger of summer. Ste. Catherine and de Maisonneuve are closed off to become huge outdoor concert halls, with outdoor stages erected from Bleury to St. Denis. Don't be too discouraged if you fail to get tickets to the the high-profile shows; the outdoor freebies are what the majority of Montrealers most look forward to. Kick back on the steps of *Place des Arts*, or on any grassy patch you can scrounge, and soak it all up day and night. Since nearly every other downtown thorough-fare becomes impassable by car, you should walk, take the metro, or bike to the site.

For those who really do want to hear jazz all year, the **Saison Jazz Montréal** (tel: 842-2667) offers a schedule of concerts between September and May at two venues (the *Salle du Gésu*, 1200 Bleury, and Lion d'Or, 1676 Ontario East). The 1996 series featured T.S. Monk, David Sanchez, and Aldo Romano, among others. Tickets were $27.95 per show.

Enjoy live jazz, along with a spectacular view of the city from the pinnacle of the world's tallest inclined tower, during **Soirées de Jazz** (tel: 252-8687). Held every Friday night at 20:00, 21:30, and 23:00 from July to September at the Salon Montréal at the top of the *Olympic Tower*, the concerts are included in the cost of ascending. This event debuted in the summer of 1996. **6**

SECRET

KARTING

Few people have the opportunity to get behind the wheel of a Formula One racer or a *Days of Thunder* stock car, but anyone can pilot a go-kart. Still, firing around the track at 50 kph in one of those tiny, open-wheel, built-to-the-ground mites feels pretty close to tooling around at 250 kph in a real car. This sport is for adults only — you must be 18 or over to participate.

There are only two circuits on the island, one indoor, one outdoor: **F1 Karting Indoor Circuit** (7054 Victoria, near Jean Talon, tel: 736-0736; Metro: Namur) and **Parc d'Amusement Anjou** (7500 Henri Bourassa East in Ville d'Anjou, between Louis H. Lafontaine and Ray Lawson, tel: 881-1915).

Musée Gilles Villeneuve (960 Gilles Villeneuve, Berthierville, tel: 514-836-2714) pays homage to Berthierville's undeniably fastest son, the late Gilles Villeneuve, whose successes first inspired Quebec's interest in F1. The enthusiast will find artifacts from his career and the world of F1 racing. Open 09:00 to 16:00 daily. **32**

SECRET

LITERATURE

Stephen Leacock, though most famous as a humorist, was a professor of economics at *McGill University* for over 35 years and the author of a history of Montreal published in 1948, *Montreal: Seaport and City*. Among his many observations about life in the city was the following remark on arts and letters: "It is not possible in such limited compass to say much of Montreal as the home of arts and letters. Nor is there much to say. No one can deny the charm of Montreal's history or the splendor of the commercial development of which it has been the center. But having brought forth a great university it does not appear to have been capable of a wider motherhood of letters and science. It has always been notoriously what is called in the Broadway offices a 'poor theatre town,' equally a 'poor lecture town.' Montreal is notoriously not a publishing town."

Well, Montreal remains something of a poor publishing town, certainly lagging far behind Toronto. But, it has a surprisingly strong English literary community, nurtured by several small presses and the Quebec Society for the Promotion of English Language Literature (QSPELL).

There are several reading series on offer, sometimes including authors from beyond Montreal, but more often exposing local talent to the public. Visitors can take in these readings, enjoy inexpensive entertainment, and be treated to insights into the city and its literary talent. Literary events and spoken-word performances abound throughout the year at **Bistro 4** (4040 St. Laurent, north of Duluth, tel: 844-6246), a charming venue at which to have a glass of wine or a local micro-brew and listen to a good story, safe from the icy weather outside. Admission is free, but many authors bring books to sell — what better souvenir than an autographed copy? Check local listings for other readings held at Bistro 4.

Each fall, the *Ritz Carlton Hotel* (1228 Sherbrooke West, tel: 845-5811) hosts the **Books & Breakfast** reading series. Held on Sunday mornings, the series attracts well-known authors hawking their latest releases. Among those who have appeared are Margaret Atwood, Mavis Gallant, Ken Dryden, and Pierre Berton. The program features three or four readers and provides an intimate setting in which to meet the writers. Breakfast is served, as well, at a cost of $21.

Several bookstores around town stage readings and launchings throughout the year, including *Chapters*, *Double Hook* (see *Secret Books* for both), and **Paragraph Bookstore and Café** (downtown at 2065 Mansfield, tel: 845-5811).

Atwater Public Library (1200 Atwater, just south of René Lévesque, tel: 935-7344; Metro: Atwater) and the **Jewish Public Library** (5151 Côte Ste. Catherine West, just west of Décarie, tel: 345-2627; Metro: Côte Ste. Catherine) have frequent readings.

The **Book Lovers Forum** review series is held every fall and spring at the **Temple Emanu-El-Beth Sholom** (395 Elm, at Sherbrooke West, in Westmount, tel: 937-3575; Metro: Atwater, Westmount Square exit). Local writers and reviewers present critical examinations of new releases, as well as revisiting some of the classics. This past season, the lectures were held Wednesday mornings at 09:30. The cost is $6, including coffee. Call ahead to verify the schedule.

Widely respected author and critic **Robert Adams** delivers a highly acclaimed book review series at *Ogilvy's* Tudor Hall (fifth floor, 1307 Ste. Catherine West, at de la Montagne). Tickets are usually sold as a series, in the fall and spring, but check whether space is available if you're only in town for a single lecture (for information, contact Robert Adams Lecture Series, 4059 Grand Blvd., Montreal, Quebec H4B 2x4, tel: 488-1152).

The very folksy **Yellow Door Coffee House** (3625 Aylmer, you can't miss its distinctive yellow door, tel: 398-6243) hosts poetry readings and has open-mike nights for those who want to try out their own compositions. Children are always welcome.

SECRET
MANSIONS

Several *walking tours* will lead you past the grand old mansions of Montreal's famed **Golden Square Mile** (in the western part of downtown, roughly from McGill University to Westmount, along Sherbrooke, in Victorian times a prestigious address). Getting inside is the problem. Following are two opportunities to venture past the front gate.

The **Mount Stephen Club** (1440 Drummond, between Ste. Catherine and de Maisonneuve, tel: 849-7338) is the only one of the grand old Square Mile mansions that you can actually enter. A private club, it is open to the public for Sunday brunch between 11:00 and 15:00 (a flat rate of $23 per person for an elegant three-course service; call for reservations). Along with your meal, you are given a guided tour of the house, which was constructed between 1880 and 1884 for George Stephen, one of the early presidents of the Bank of Montreal and a founder of the Canadian Pacific Railway. Brunch is served in the mansion's original dining room, granting visitors a genuine taste of the lifestyle of the Victorian rich and famous. Exquisitely appointed with luxurious bird's-eye maple, Cuban mahogany, British Columbia redwood, Indian lemon tree, and English walnut, as well as hand-painted stained glass depicting scenes from Shakespeare and 22-carat gold door handles and hinges, the house is a monument to 19th-century craftsmanship and extravagance. Interestingly, the house was a private residence until 1925, at which time it was taken over for the exclusive, private club it is today. In 1975 it was designated a historic monument. This is a very worthwhile splurge, for the culinary delights as well as for the tour. ㉝

The **Masonic Memorial Temple** (Sherbrooke West, corner of St. Marc, entry via 2295 St. Marc, tel: 933-6739 or 933-6730) was built in 1929 in memory of those who fell in World War I and it opened for its first lodge meeting in February 1930. The Grand Lodge of Quebec is one of the more impressive and imposing monuments along the Golden Mile. For the past five years, the Masons have offered free guided tours of the temple (donations are solicited, though not required), usually during the last two weeks in August when none of the lodges are in session. This tour offers a rare opportunity for an outsider to penetrate the mysterious world of

Freemasonry, and to actually see the symbol-laden chambers where the Masons hold their meetings. The tours are guided by Masons who are only too happy to explain the principles of the fraternity and the meaning behind its several rites. The mystique of the society makes this tour quite an experience. It is recommended that you call ahead to ensure that the tours are being offered when you are available to take them. Usually, they are given between 10:00 and 15:30, but they are very informal and may be postponed without notice on any given day. ㉞

SECRET

MCGILL

McGill University (845 Sherbrooke West, tel: 398-4455; Metro: McGill), one of Canada's most venerable and venerated institutions of learning, marked its 175th anniversary in 1996. The grandly domed **Arts Building**, which dominates the main campus and commands a view down McGill College, dates from 1839 and is the oldest of the university's buildings. At the foot of the building is the tomb of the university's founder, James McGill. Many people stroll past, and even across, the campus, but don't be shy about entering its buildings and wandering the hallowed halls of academe. ㉗

The **McGill Welcome Centre** (Burnside Hall, just inside and east of the main gates, on the ground floor, tel: 398-6555) is the place to go to arrange for a free, hour-long guided campus tour. They

are offered all year and will be conducted whenever requested, even for just one person. Simply call a few days in advance to set up an appointment. The guides are McGill students, and they know all the nooks and crannies of the campus. Open weekdays 09:00 to 17:00.

Redpath Museum (just below and to the west of the Arts Building, tel: 398-4086) is a natural-history museum housing the various archaeological, palaeontological, botanical, and geological relics collected by the university's researchers over the years. Open Monday to Thursday 09:00 to 17:00 and Sunday 13:00 to 17:00 from June to September, and Monday to Friday 09:00 to 17:00 from September to June.

Campus visitors with a macabre bent should see *Secret Cadavers*.

SECRET
MILITARY

The **Musée d'Histoire Militaire de Montréal** (6560 Hochelaga, corner of Langelier, east of the *Olympic Stadium*, tel: 252-2777 ext. 2241), located on the Canadian Forces Base in Longue Pointe, is so well hidden, it's not even listed in the phone book, despite having been in existence since 1962. Not a national secret, just the victim of a nonexistent advertising budget. Dedicated to the Royal Canadian Ordnance Corps, the museum houses over 8,000 pieces of military memorabilia, including munitions, insignia, medals, tanks, small arms, parachutes, and captured enemy materiel. Their prize possession is a Maxim heavy machine gun from 1892. Open Wednesday through Sunday 10:00 to 16:00. Free admission and parking. ㉟

Several other small regimental museums are to be found around Montreal, including those listed below. These museums are likely to be of interest primarily to the military buff, rather than the generalist. Opening hours are sometimes limited, so call ahead before visiting.

Black Watch of Canada Regimental Museum and Archives (2067 Bleury, tel: 496-1686; Metro: Place des Arts).

Les Fusiliers Mont Royal Regimental Museum (3721 Henri-Julien, tel: 283-7444).

Canadian Grenadier Guards Regimental Museum (4171 Esplanade, tel: 496-1984).

Royal Montreal Regiment Museum (4625 Ste. Catherine West, Westmount, tel: 496-2003).

S E C R E T
MONEY

La Bourse, the *Montreal Stock Exchange* (800 Square Victoria, tel: 871-2424; Metro: Square Victoria), has a visitors' gallery on the fourth floor. Newly renovated for the fall of 1996, it is open Monday to Friday 09:00 to 17:00. Though not one of the major exchanges, the Bourse features all the frenetic action that characterizes the making and losing of fortunes in the blink of an eye or the desperate wag of a finger. Admission to the gallery is free. ❽

One is pretty well obliged to take a peek inside the **Bank of Montreal** on Place d'Armes. With its marble, its columns, its vaulted ceiling, and its huge expanse, it seems to be more mausoleum than bank, a sarcophagus of wealth and power. ❸

Once the awe inspired by this 1847 structure wears off, turn to your left immediately past the entrance and take a quick look at the **Money Museum** (119 St. Jacques West, tel: 877-6892; Metro: Place d'Armes). An attendant is present to explain the exhibit, which includes a replica of the first cashier's window, old banknotes, and counterfeit currency. Open during bank hours, Monday to Friday (excluding holidays) 10:00 to 16:00; during July and August it is closed between 12:00 and 13:00. Admission is free.

SECRET

MOUNT ROYAL

Writing about his visit to Montreal in 1914, Sir Arthur Conan Doyle described his first experience of **Mount Royal**: "On the first day we ascended the mountain and looked down on what is one of the most wonderful views in the world — and I can speak now with some knowledge. At your feet lies the old gray town, which is spreading fast upon either flank, and which is impressive in its wealth of domes and spires. . . . It is no mushroom city this. It contains buildings which would be considered venerable and historical even by a European standard." ㉘

The design for Mount Royal park was laid out in 1874 by Frederick Law Olmsted, whose landscaping achievements included New York's Central Park and the Capitol Grounds in Washington, DC. Of Mount Royal, Laws said, "The opportunity and advantages for producing certain charms of natural scenery are such as are possessed by no other city in any ground held for a public park."

Montrealers think they know the mountain just because they see it every day. If ever they took the time to really explore this treasure trove, they'd be shocked by all the hidden riches. For the artistically inclined, there are 11 sculptures, dating from a 1964 symposium, scattered between *Beaver Lake* and the Chalet. **Smith House** (situated at the second parking lot past *Beaver Lake*, coming from the west) was built in 1858 by merchant Hosea Bonen Smith as a retreat from the bustle and congestion of the city. It has been declared a heritage site and can be toured for free on Sundays at 13:30 in August and September (the tour takes about an hour). *Mount Royal Revisited* is a small book that can be purchased ($3.50) at Smith House to lead you on a self-guided walking tour. Every Sunday in September, **Les Amis de la Montagne** guide an all-day walking tour called "Les Trois Soumets," to the three summits of the mountain (Westmount, Outremont, and the central peak). Leaving from the Sir George Étienne Cartier monument at du Parc and Mont Royal, on the eastern slope, at 10:00 and returning at

16:30, the tour costs $7. You're guaranteed to finish it knowing all there is to know about Montreal's centerpiece (for information on this and other events, call 844-4928).

Drop by the Sir George Étienne Cartier monument on du Parc, just south of Mont Royal, on a Sunday afternoon when the weather is warm and take in the retro-hippie revival of the **Tam Tam Jam**. What began several years ago as an impromptu gathering of all manner of drummer and percussionist has evolved into a highly organized session, complete with food vendors. For those who have witnessed the evolution of the jam, there is something rather contrived about the pseudospontaneity of it now. Still, it's not something you see everywhere, it's free, and sometimes it even sounds good. ㊱

For those interested in a little cinematic trivia, the path that wends its way up the east side of the mountain from the Cartier monument is the very path Michael Douglas ran in a scene from *Running*, a film about an American marathoner preparing for the 1976 Olympic Games.

At the foot of the mountain, at the west end, is **Notre Dame des Neiges** cemetery, the largest Catholic cemetery in North America: one square mile, with one million interred. Pick up a map to the historic burial sites at the main entrance on Côte des Neiges. Just around the corner, at 5085 Decelles, is the oldest house in the Côte des Neiges district. Built in 1713, it serves as the home of the cemetery manager. It is made of stone with a tin roof, and features distinctive rooftop extensions that acted as fire breaks. These were characteristic of the era, as Montreal had suffered several huge blazes that destroyed entire sections of the city. Also impressive for its older monuments is **Mount Royal Cemetery**, the Protestant cemetery situated a little further up the mountain along Chemin Remembrance. ㉗

SECRET
MUSEUMS

Although the **Canadian Centre for Architecture** (1920 Baile, just north of René Lévesque at St. Marc, tel: 939-7026; Metro: Guy-Concordia) is hardly hidden after more than 15 acclaimed years, this grand museum on the art and science of architecture demands listing because it is unique to Montreal. The museum, itself an excellent example of the exploitation of space and light, consists of a new building that embraces the historic 1874 Shaughnessy House, set in a primly manicured garden. Don't miss the exquisite tea room with its modern furniture and classical woodwork. Open October to May, Wednesday to Friday 11:00 to 18:00, Thursday 11:00 to 20:00, Saturday and Sunday 11:00 to 17:00; June to September, Tuesday to Sunday 11:00 to 18:00, Thursday 11:00 to 20:00. Adults $5, students and seniors $3. ㊳

For those who are interested in Montreal's religious underpinnings, the **Mother House of the Sisters of Charity of Montreal** (1185 St. Mathieu, just south of the Faubourg Ste. Catherine, tel: 937-9501; Metro: Guy-Concordia), known as the Grey Nuns, houses the **Marguerite d'Youville Centre**, a museum dedicated to the memory of Mother d'Youville and the history of the order.

She was the administrator of the original General Hospital, which was situated at what is now Carré d'Youville in Old Montreal. The museum contains the remains of Marguerite d'Youville, relics and furniture from the original Mother House dating from the 18th century, and a crypt where 260 sisters of the order are laid to rest. Guided tours are offered Wednesday through Sunday between 13:30 and 15:00. **39**

In conjunction with the city's 350th anniversary in 1992, the hidden little **Musée des Hospitalières de l'Hôtel Dieu** (201 des Pins West, corner of Jeanne Mance, tel: 849-2919) was opened, dedicated to presenting the contributions of the Hospitallers of St. Joseph community to the city. Stored herein are letters and artifacts relating to the original Hôtel Dieu, Montreal's first hospital, which lend insight into early medical practices. The original Hôtel Dieu, erected in 1642 in Old Montreal, is long gone. The museum stands immediately to the west of the modernized hospital, built in 1860 on the corner of des Pins and St. Urbain. At the time, it was among the most modern medical facilities in the British Empire. Immediately west of the museum is the chapel (209 des Pins), also built in 1860. Tours are not available, but daily mass is celebrated at 16:00. The museum's treasure is a staircase, dating from 1634, from the original Hôtel Dieu of La Flèche, given to Montreal by the Department of Sarthe, France. Open mid-June to mid-October, Tuesday to Friday 10:00 to 17:00, Saturday and Sunday 13:00 to 17:00; mid-October to mid-June, Wednesday to Sunday 13:00 to 17:00. Admission $5 for adults. **40**

Founded in 1979, the **Montreal Holocaust Memorial Centre** (5151 Côte Ste. Catherine, between Décarie and Victoria, tel: 345-2605; Metro: Côte Ste. Catherine) was the first Holocaust educational institution established in Canada. Montreal, which has the largest survivor population in North America, is a fitting location. The permanent exhibition, entitled *Splendour and Destruction*, documents the diverse and vibrant Jewish community that existed across Europe, and traces its struggle from 1919, through the Nazis' concerted effort to wipe it out, until the affirmation of hope marked by its ultimate survival. The artifacts focus on the dignity with which Jews endured Nazi atrocities and the humanity they retained under inhuman conditions. As my guide put it, "The memorial doesn't talk about Nazis, but about Jews." And it does so with moving simplicity. Far from being the world's largest Holocaust memorial, it stands as a stirring tribute to the suffering of the millions. Go out of your way to see it and to learn. Literally a hidden museum, it is located in the basement of the Édifice Cummings. The museum is open Sunday to Thursday 10:00 to 16:00. Admission is free.

Musée des Pompiers Auxiliaires de Montréal (5100 St. Laurent, corner of Laurier) is dedicated to the history of one of the most dangerous of professions — fire fighting. The museum serves up a collection of photographs of some of Montreal's most spectacular blazes, old fire-fighting equipment that contrasts with the photos of modern trucks, memorabilia, old helmets, toy trucks, and a wall dedicated to firemen who lost their lives on the job. Members of the auxiliary will gladly guide you through the exhibit, which includes a demonstration of the old manual alarm system, a voodoo tangle of lights and bells and switches and teletype that will leave you amazed that firemen ever made it to the scene before 911 and computer-aided dispatch. The museum is situated in a fire station that was constructed in 1903 to serve as the city hall for St.

Louis de Mile End, when it was an independent town. Open only on Sundays, between 14:00 and 17:00. Admission is free, although donations to the Auxiliary Firefighters are welcomed. **41**

The small display at **Maison de la Poste** (in the Canada Post building at the corner of St. Jacques and Peel, entry via St. Jacques; Metro: Bonaventure) is a must-see for philatelists, containing commemorative stamps and various collectibles sold by Canada Post. Collectors can pick up a unique souvenir here, or just browse through the material. Open regular business hours Monday to Friday. Admission is free. **42**

La Ferme St. Gabriel (2146 Place Dublin, off Favard in Pointe St. Charles, tel: 935-8136) is one of the oldest buildings in Montreal, and one of the few that dates to the French regime. Reconstructed in 1698 following a fire, the building's original structure dates to 1668. The farmhouse now holds a museum with artifacts from the period, documenting the life and times of Marguerite Bourgeoys (1620–1700), founder of the Congregation of Notre Dame in Montreal. She was instrumental in the founding of the Church of Notre Dame de Bonsecours, and in 1658 she established Montreal's first girls school. According to Stephen Leacock, her works in Ville Marie are held in reverence surpassed only by Jeanne Mance. Bourgeoys was canonized in 1982. Guided tours are available from mid-April to mid-December, Tuesday to Saturday from 13:30 to 15:00 and Sunday at 13:30, 14:30, and 15:30.

Visiting Ferme St. Gabriel provides a good excuse for going into one of the city's less visited districts, **Pointe St. Charles**. Among the oldest working-class neighborhoods in Montreal, this area in the late 1800s was the core of the city's industrial development. Bearing testimony to that fact are the criss-crossing rail tracks that pass over it like scars. Although a walk through the Pointe is a journey through much of Montreal's industrial history, many structures that once were architecturally sumptuous have unfortunately fallen into disrepair as tenements. There has been little gentrification in the district. Isolated Rue Sebastapol has the oldest examples of workers' row houses still standing — just barely, however, as only two of the quadriplexes are occupied, while the rest are boarded up and in poor repair.

The brand new **Écomusée du Fier Monde** (2050 Amherst, between Ontario and Sherbrooke, directly across from the *Marché St. Jacques*, tel: 528-8444; Metro: Beaudry), which opened in October 1996, pays tribute to the working classes of industrial, poverty-stricken south-central Montreal. In contrast to historical markers of the fabled *Golden Square Mile* of the industrial giants, Fier Monde uses photographs, video, and maps to trace the lives of the underclasses, so often neglected when the history of urban development is recounted. There is also an exhibit on the history of public baths, paying homage to the Bain Généreux, the 1926 art-deco bath that has been converted to house the museum. A note for unilingual visitors: except for the baths display, the museum's exhibits are all described in French — a distinct problem, since the written narrative pulls the whole thing together. Open Wednesday 11:00 to 20:00, Thursday to Sunday 10:30 to 17:00. Adults $4, students and seniors $3. ㉑

SECRET
MUSIC

Cheap Thrills (1433 Bishop, tel: 844-7604; Metro: Guy-Concordia; a second downtown location is at 2044 Metcalfe, tel: 844-8988; Metro: Peel) is the place to go for a varied selection of used discs.

L'Échange (3694 St. Denis, north of des Pins, tel: 849-1913) has good prices on used discs and books.

Chin Phat (1448 Peel, tel: 284-5773; Metro: Peel) is Montreal central for hip-hop CDs.

HMV (1035 Ste. Catherine West, corner of Peel, tel: 844-0269; Metro: Peel) is the megastore. Volume buying lets this establishment offer the price to beat on new releases. Also available is a good selection of videos.

SECRET
NATIVE CULTURE

Kahnawake, the Mohawk territory just south of Montreal (take the Mercier Bridge to the 132 exit, turn left at the first traffic light, tel: 638-9699), is too often neglected by tourists. Native culture is an integral part of Canadian history, and Kahnawake gives visitors an opportunity to experience some of its richness. *Mohawk Trail Walking Tours* (tel: 635-7289) offer a good introduction to the territory. ❹❸

An exhibit on the history and culture of the Iroquois Confederacy and the village of Kahnawake is installed at the **Cultural Centre**. The staff are well versed in native lore and are happy to lead visitors around the center. Open Monday to Friday 10:00 to 18:00. A donation of $3 per person is suggested.

The main rectory at **Mission St. Francis Xavier** dates to 1717. The museum houses religious artifacts and documents relating to the history of this Catholic mission. The Kateri Center honors the Blessed Kateri Tekakwitha (1656–80), whose tomb is in the right transept of the church. Open weekdays 10:00 to 12:00 and 13:00 to 17:00, Saturday and Sunday 10:00 to 17:00.

Powwow (tel: 632-8667) is held every July and is without doubt the largest attraction of the year, drawing natives and nonnatives to the territory. Call for this year's schedule. Other native dance troupes perform at Kahnawake and elsewhere throughout the summer, notably the Eagle Wing Dancers (tel: 635-5194 or 632-7674) and the Keepers of the Eastern Door (tel: 638-6521).

Several galleries in Montreal celebrate the beauty of native arts and crafts, including **Canadian Guild of Crafts** (2025 Peel, tel: 849-6091; Metro: Peel) and **Red Cedar Gallery** (6127 Monkland, tel: 489-8644; Metro: Villa Maria).

SECRET

NATURE PARKS

The **Montreal Urban Community's Nature Park Network** (Administration Services, 2580 St. Joseph East, tel: 280-6700) is one of the genuine hidden treasures of the island. Too many Montrealers seem to be oblivious to the fact that they inhabit an island, that their habitat is encircled by a waterfront. Admittedly, much of the St. Lawrence River and Rivière des Prairies is far too polluted to be enjoyed, but there is, nonetheless, something soothing about being near a large body of water. Recognizing the value of preserving green spaces, and realizing that, once lost, valuable ecosystems cannot be recuperated, the MUC commenced in 1979 to develop nature preserves. There are currently six parks in the network, each one offering a paradise for hikers, bikers, and cross-country skiers, or simply an opportunity to put a little grass under your feet. Access to the parks is free, except for a parking fee of $3 for the entire day. All of the parks are open year round.

Parc Nature de la Pointe aux Prairies is at the eastern extreme of the island, where the two rivers meet. The forested area off Sherbrooke East is the only mature forest in the city's east end, a lush grove of maple, basswood, oak, and ash, offering a cool oasis on hot summer days and sheltered trails for winter excursions. The most unique feature of Pointe aux Prairies is the network of marshes in the sector off Gouin East, not to be missed by bird-watchers. Trails lead right through the marshes, providing marvelous viewing points. Being the furthest from residential neighborhoods, this

is the least heavily used of the nature parks, and it gives the visitor a refreshing sense of being far from the city. **44**

Off the main Sherbrooke entrance can be found the **Hawthorne-Dale Cemetery**. Tombs here are not exceptionally old — dating from World War 1 — but it is unusual to find an English cemetery at the eastern extremity of the island.

Parc Nature de l'Île de la Visitation is more akin to an urban park than a nature park. Located in Ahuntsic, accessible from Gouin, this small tract on the Rivière des Prairies offers walking and cycling paths (these link up with the bike path that runs along Gouin through the city). Fish-eating birds congregate along the Hydro Quebec dam to hunt in the shallows. **45**

Parc Nature Bois de Liesse is perhaps the most accessible of the parks, situated off Autoroute 13 in St. Laurent. It is renowned for its *bois francs*, valuable hardwood stands, and the nature trails permit you to escape deep into these peaceful woods. **46**

Parc Nature du Bois de l'Île-Bizard, on Île Bizard in Lac des Deux Montagnes, offers the greatest variety of activity and ecological diversity. A small sandy beach is the prime summertime attraction. After cooling off with a swim, walk through forest and marshland to watch the birds, see the beaver dams, enjoy the flora, and, generally, experience the tranquillity. **47**

Parc Nature du Cap St. Jacques, the largest of the parks, is located off Gouin in Pierrefonds, on a peninsula jutting into Lac des Deux Montagnes on one side, where lies a popular beach, and the Rivière des Prairies on the other. Because of the prevailing winds, this is a favorite windsurfing spot. The Ecological Farm is

a must for children, with its animals and freshly grown produce
— the latter is on sale at the General Store. Be forewarned that
because of its popularity, the Cap can be very crowded on summer
weekends, so arrive early if you intend to stake out a spot on the
beach. All beaches in the nature parks have lifeguards on duty, and
authorities had the sense to outlaw the use of boom-boxes. **48**

Parc Nature de l'Anse à l'Orme, just west of Cap St. Jacques,
is a narrow strip of forest leading to a boat-launching ramp on
Lac des Deux Montagnes. More exposed than the Cap, this, too is
an excellent windsurfing area. **49**

Except for l'Anse à l'Orme, all the parks have visitor information
centers, where you will find pamphlets explaining the particular-
ities of the park, as well as naturalists, who will be happy to point
out things to look for on your hikes or cycling tours. There are
also a variety of expositions, organized activities, and nature walks
throughout the year. Canoe and sea-kayaking adventures take
place periodically during the summer.

I've mentioned summer and winter activities, but don't forget
the fall. There's no need to travel any further than the forests of
the nature parks to witness the spectacular changing of the leaves.
Outings are generally conducted in French and English. When
seeking information, specify the language in which you need
service. For information on the entire range of activities available
in Montreal's nature parks, contact the Administrative Services for
the Nature Park Network.

SECRET

NEIGHBORHOODS

The **Plateau Mont Royal** is a fascinating part of the city (Metro: Mont Royal). One of the most ethnically diverse quarters, it is also a trendy, gentrified neighborhood populated by many members of the artistic community. Stroll down Mont Royal east from du Parc. It is a cluttered cornucopia of thrift shops, specialty stores, cafés, and restaurants — not chains, but establishments exclusive to the Plateau, very much conceived with the needs of local residents in mind. This pleasant commercial/residential mix stretches all the way to de Lorimier. Don't rush to see anything in particular, but linger, browse, savor a café au lait served in a deep bowl, as in Paris. In an effort to draw in more tourists, the district has established its own tourism authority (tel: 848-0099). They have a kiosk right outside the Mont Royal Metro station, across the street from the *Maison de la Culture* on Mont Royal, east of St. Denis. If you're exploring the area on your own, this is a worthwhile first stop so you can pick up maps and find out about local happenings.

Mordecai Richler, acclaimed novelist and — more recently — separatist-baiter, often draws upon Montreal as a setting for his work. In an interview for a *National Film Board* biography, entitled *The Apprenticeship of Mordecai Richler*, he described the advantages of writing about Canada: "We're charting a territory for the first time, so when you're describing Montreal it's not like somebody else now sitting down to describe London, which has been described so well so many times before. And it is an exotic background in many ways." He grew up in the old Jewish neighborhood, at the western end of the Plateau, roughly between du Parc to the west and St. Laurent to the east, and south from Bernard to Mont Royal. This is the Montreal of Richler's youth. His family moved into a cold-water flat at 5257 St. Urbain in 1938, when he was seven, and remained at that address for 10 years. If you attend a show at *Club Soda* on du Parc, know that you are on the site of what used to be the pool hall where Richler passed much of his youth. Duddy Kravitz (*The Apprenticeship of Duddy Kravitz*), Jake Hersh (*St. Urbain's Horseman*), and Joshua Shapiro (*Joshua Then and Now*) all spent their formative years in this district. The early Jewish immigrants have now largely dispersed from here, the notable exception being the Hasidic community, which straddles both sides of du Parc. The best bagels in town are to be found at the emporiums along Fairmount or St. Viateur (in both cases between du Parc and St. Laurent). Among several upstarts, the grand masters of the craft are the **Bagel Factory** (74 Fairmount West) and the **Bagel Shop** (263 and 158 St. Viateur West). Both of these establishments are open 24 hours a day. Select any one of dozens of *Greek restaurants* for some of the best souvlaki in town.

Promenade Ontario runs along Ontario East between Pie 1x and St. Germain. Get away from the central retail streets of the downtown core and the sterility of the shopping mall to browse through this quarter, part of *Hochelaga-Maisonneuve*. It's an opportunity to see working-class, French Canadian Montreal. As you stroll, you won't be jostled by other foreigners. As in the *Plateau*, at ground level, some of the stores may appear run down, but look up and you'll be dazzled by the old-style architecture these structures preserve. 🎟

Indeed, *Hochelaga-Maisonneuve* is one of the oldest quarters of the city, and is interesting because it was always an industrial, working-class area. The wealthy merchants immediately moved west from the original settlement, while factories and employees who couldn't afford cross-town transportation gravitated to the east. The centerpiece of the neighborhood is now the *Olympic Stadium*. At one time, Maisonneuve was a separate city from Montreal. Its old city hall is now the Bibliothèque Maisonneuve, on the corner of Hochelaga and Pie ix. Still in place in the library is the very chair that was used by the mayor during council meetings. One of the things that makes this section of town so fascinating is the intricate architecture of the dwellings that were occupied by the working poor of past centuries.

Little Italy lies east of St. Laurent, just south of Jean Talon (Metro: Jean Talon). Make sure to walk in this neighborhood at a time of day when your system can absorb an intake of high-octane coffee and high-calorie pastries. Also, check out the **Madonna della Difensa Church** (6810 Henri Julien, south of Jean Talon East, at Dante). On display is the only statue (to anyone's knowledge) of Mussolini in the city. It is a remnant of the days when he was admired more for his facility with train schedules than despised for everything else he did. *Amarage* (tel: 272-7049) conducts guided walking tours of the area on selected dates in the summer and fall.

Monkland Avenue in **Notre Dame de Grâce** (Metro: Villa Maria), between Girouard and Harvard, used to be a rather dowdy commercial strip, but it has become a lively stretch of trendy cafés, bars, and restaurants, most of which boast terraces for outdoor dining when weather permits. Monkland is a relaxing alternative to the crush of downtown, promising a nice getaway for a quiet meal or drink, as well as a chance to become acquainted with the kind of neighborhood spirit that can still flourish in a big city. Few tourists venture out to this district of tree-lined streets, but it is easily accessible by metro (the Villa Maria station is situated on Monkland and Décarie, a couple of blocks to the east) or car (from downtown, just take Sherbrooke west to Girouard, then turn right and proceed north to Monkland). The choice of fare here is exceptionally eclectic: from Lebanese to Ethiopian to Italian to Chinese to North American pub meals. A lunchtime or evening visit is therefore recommended.

Ste. Anne de Bellevue, located at the extreme western tip of the island (take either Highway 20 or 40 and follow the signs, or drive along scenic Chemin Bord du Lac all the way from Lachine), has a quaint downtown core with a small-town New England feeling. Ste. Anne, the main thoroughfare, is lined with pubs, restaurants, and specialty shops. Even the residents seem like tourists as they stroll aimlessly, pretending to be away from home. Check out the G. D'Aoust Department Store (73 Ste. Anne), a throw-back multipurpose shop. It is purposefully retro. You won't hear the blare of an intercom to page personnel. Instead, interdepartmental messages are sent whipping overhead along exposed tubes that criss-cross the ceiling. The store is stocked with excellent gift ideas, as well as clothes and household articles. Running parallel to Ste. Anne, right up to the Ste. Anne Locks, is the boardwalk, along which many restaurants have set up outdoor terraces. Watch the boats come and go, and curse the roar of the jet-skis. **⓱**

Westmount is an area with which tourists are well acquainted because of the *Golden Square Mile*, trendy Greene Avenue (west of

Atwater, running south from Sherbrooke; Metro: Atwater, West-mount Square exit), and beautiful Westmount Park (8 blocks west of Greene). But the most elaborate of the residential mansions are situated in Upper Westmount. *Summit Circle* is the pinnacle of the neighborhood. The graciously curving streets that mount the hill are lined with spectacular homes. There is parking at the Circle if you want to drive up, enjoy the view, and then stroll around, without having to climb the entire way up. Novelist/poet/recording artist Leonard Cohen is Westmount's most internation-ally acclaimed artistic product. Cohen was reared in the house at 599 Belmont, graduated from Westmount High on Ste. Catherine, and attended synagogue as a youth at the Shaar Hashomayim on Côte St. Antoine. He would later attend McGill and haunt the coffeehouses that surrounded the campus in the 1950s.

S E C R E T

OUTINGS

An annual event held on *Île Notre Dame* in early August, **Les Fêtes Gourmandes Internationales** (tel: 861-8241; Metro: Île Ste. Hélène) is a veritable culinary travelogue, boasting nearly 500 dishes from all five continents. Have a Polynesian specialty, fol-lowed by some African or Laotian fare, or even some home-bred exotica like ostrich or caribou. Or, how about taking a chunk out of a shark before one takes a chunk out of you? In the same vein, you may choose to chow down on a heap of alligator stew. Entrance to the site costs $4; then there is a reasonable cost per plate. Call for information on festival dates and the exact coordinates. **16**

An interesting and unusual way to pass the time is to watch cases being tried at the **Palais de Justice** (Metro: Place d'Armes). Montreal's old court house, at 155 Notre Dame East, just east of St. Laurent, built in 1856 by the celebrated Montreal architect John Ostell, became obsolete and was replaced in 1923 by the building at 100 Notre Dame East, designed by Ernest Cormier. Trials are now held in a typically nondescript modern tower, at 1 Notre Dame East, right at the corner of St. Laurent. The experience will be especially interesting for non-Canadian legal buffs interested in exposure to our system of justice. If nothing else, you come away shaking your head at how unlike *L.A. Law* — or even *Street Legal* — the real thing is. A large board in the front lobby lists the day's docket and the chamber in which each case is to be heard. Trials are conducted in either official language, sometimes both simultaneously, so you may want to pick a defendant with an English-sounding name as that case is most likely to be heard in English. **51**

CBC/Radio Canada (1400 René Lévesque East, east of Berri, tel: 597-7787; Metro: Beaudry) provides tours of the Quebec headquarters of Canada's national broadcaster. Guides will lead you through radio and television studios, as well as a museum devoted to the history of broadcasting. Visit sets, see where they are constructed, and get up close and personal with props. If you're lucky enough to link up with a small group, you might even be brought into the actual newsroom or the studios of RDI, Canada's

French-language news channel. The tour takes about an hour and a half. It is only available to groups, but the CBC is happy to allow individuals to tag along, and will even try to find one that is compatible with your needs (in other words, you won't be forced to join a class of moody 14 year olds). Groups of less than 20 pay $50, 20 to 60 pay $100, and 60 to 90 pay $175. An individual joining a group pays only $2.50. Tours are given nearly every weekday at 10:00 and 14:00 (depending upon demand), in either English or French. Call in advance whether you are booking for yourself or a group.

See all that surrounds the mounting of major stage productions and concerts in a 90-minute behind-the-scenes tour of **Place des Arts** (260 de Maisonneuve West, west of St. Laurent, tel: 842-2112 for ticket info, 285-4275 for tour info; Metro: Place des Arts). Unfortunately, tours are available only to groups of 15 or more ($6.50 per adult, $5 for students and seniors). If you're alone, call anyway; if a group has been scheduled, you may be able to tag along. Group tours can be arranged on request for any day of the week, between 09:00 and 15:00. Requests should be submitted a week in advance. 52

Take a tour of the ***Olympic Stadium*** (4545 Pierre de Coubertin, corner of Pie IX, tel: 252-8687; Metro: Pie IX), the greatest white elephant in Canadian history. The stadium is the grossest example of financial excess and poor planning accessible to the public. Keep your eyes peeled for tears in the artificial turf that are the scourge of every athlete ever to play there, and for cracks in the concrete that are the terror of every fan who has ever attended a game (just kidding — it's been well over a year since any significant chunk of concrete has fallen off). To go to the summit of the tower, enter at 3200 Viau (Metro: Viau), at the east end of the stadium. Open 10:00 to 18:00, 10:00 to 21:00 from 15 June to 2 September. ❻

The **LaSalle Car Festival** (tel: 595-7787), an annual August weekend gathering of car buffs in the Parc des Rapides on Boulevard Lasalle, is a great occasion to gawk at all the classics you've dreamed of owning, but probably never will.

For the participation-minded, **Horizon Roc** (2350 Dickson, tel: 899-5000) is the largest interior climbing center in Canada. They offer courses as well as climbing opportunities for those with experience.

Guided tours of **Station d'Épuration des Eaux Usées** (12001 Maurice Duplessis, corner of St. Jean Baptiste, north of Sherbrooke, south of Gouin, in the far east end, tel: 280-4400), Montreal's water-treatment facility, were scheduled to commence in January 1997. At the time of writing, the schedule was unavailable, so call ahead. Learn what a large urban center does with its sludge and scum (those are the technical terms for all that stuff we flush and dump).

SECRET

PARKS
(OFF ISLAND)

As an alternative to the various *nature parks* on the island, there are several provincial parks located off island, but still very accessible.

Hiking, biking, and a beach are the primary attractions at **Oka Park**, located northwest of the city (access from Highway 640 or 344, tel: 514-479-8365). The Oka Calvary features 5.5 km of trails passing four oratories and three chapels, dating to 1742, along the Stations of the Cross. The Grande Baie trail is 3 km long, and crosses four distinct ecosystems. **9**

Îles de Boucherville (access from Highway 20, tel: 514-928-5088 in summer, 514-928-5089 in winter), a string of islands in the St. Lawrence east of Montreal, connected by wooden footbridges, is a good place for birders to view Canada geese, ospreys, and blue herons. **53**

Apple trees and birds are the most prominent features of **Mont St. Bruno**, just south of Montreal (access from Highways 30, 20, or 116). Spread out around a mountain, this park is a favorite *cross-country ski* retreat in the winter. **54**

S E C R E T

POLITICS

For a brief period (1843–49), Montreal was the capital of Canada.
The Parliament building stood at what is now **Place d'Youville**
(in the heart of *Old Montreal*, just north of *Pointe à Callière*;
Metro: Place d'Armes). It was burned during a riot in 1849, and
as a result, Montreal was deemed too volatile to serve as the seat
of government. **55**

During this period, the Governor General, the Crown's repre-
sentative in Canada, resided at what is now the central building
of **Villa Maria Convent** (at the eastern extremity of Monkland,
immediately east of Décarie; Metro: Villa Maria). At the time, the
manor house, sitting on a large parcel of land known as Monk-
lands, had been the residence of James Monk, Chief Justice of the
District of Montreal and Speaker of the Legislature of Lower
Canada. This site marks a good starting point for a stroll west
along *Monkland*, which has developed in recent years into a lively
neighborhood gathering place, thanks to the opening of several
cafés and restaurants, most of which have outdoor terraces for
summertime relaxation. The grounds are lovely and you can stroll
around, but the building serves as a high school and is not open
for public visits.

Montreal's city hall, or **Hôtel de Ville** (275 Notre Dame East,
above Place Jacques Cartier, tel: 872-3355; Metro: Place d'Armes),
was originally designed in 1878 by Henri Maurice Perrault, drawing inspiration from the Hôtel de Ville of Paris and the Palais du

Commerce of Rennes. All but the exterior facade was gutted by fire in 1922, but it was reopened in February 1926. Sometimes called the "municipal palace," this may refer more to the monarchical style of some of Montreal's mayors than to the architecture. Buffs of more modern Quebec history will be interested to know that it was from the second-floor balcony of this building on 9 May 1967, that France's President Charles de Gaulle, in a fit of Gallic passion, cried out, "Vive le Québec! Vive le Québec libre!" There has been much debate as to whether or not de Gaulle intended to inflame nationalist fervor, but that was the effect. Quebec's then nascent sovereignist movement was boosted by the implication that the French motherland sympathized with its quest for independence, an issue still of not inconsiderable import in Canada-France relations. **56**

Tours of the Hôtel de Ville are offered every hour, and take approximately 30 minutes. However, for a different experience, go to the public gallery and attend an actual sitting of the City Council; call ahead to confirm that council is in session when you intend to visit. The debates can be tedious or raucous, depending on the issues at hand. Most of the proceedings are conducted in French, but there are several English counselors and they may speak in English. Similarly, during the sessions when public consultations are held and questions from residents are considered, issues may be discussed in English.

SECRET

POOL

The stick-and-cue-ball kind, not the get-wet kind. The pool-hall trend seems to have eased of late, but some of the establishments still stand. *Bacci* (two locations: 4205 St. Denis, tel: 844-3929; and 3553 St. Laurent, tel: 287-9331) is definitely upscale, while **Sharx Pool Bar** (in the Faubourg Ste. Catherine, 1606 Ste. Catherine West, corner of Guy, tel: 934-3105; Metro: Guy-Concordia) is one of the biggest. You gotta love the revisionist spelling of **Q-Stix** (4158 St. Laurent, tel: 847-0086), which seems to be a requirement of the contemporary pool hall. **Jilly's** (inside Decor Décarie, 6900 Décarie, south of Jean Talon; Metro: Namur), not content to be simply a pool hall, bar, and pinball arcade, is now featuring Internet and computer game terminals.

SECRET

RELIGION

Writing in 1869, American author Harriet Beecher Stowe referred somewhat reverentially to Montreal as "a most religious city . . . Montreal is a mountain of churches. Every shade and form of faith is here well represented in wood or stone, and the gospel feast set forth in every form and shape to suit the spiritual appetite of all inquirers."

Rather less reverentially, in an address given in December 1881 at the Windsor Hotel (now an office complex and home of the Piment Rouge at 1170 Peel, opposite Dominion Square), Mark Twain said: "This is the first time I was ever in a city where you couldn't throw a brick without breaking a church window. Yet I was told that you were going to build one more; I said the scheme is good, but where are you going to find room? They said, we will build it on top of another church and use an elevator."

Tourists flock to the most renowned and centrally located of the multitude of holy places: *Notre Dame Cathedral*, Marie Reine du Monde, and Christ Church Cathedral. And, indeed, these are musts. While some cities' histories were driven by war or the arts or commerce or politics, Montreal's has been powered by religion. Much of its early settlement was financed by missionary orders. Sulpicians and Jesuits were prominent among the city's founders. If you're interested in the religious dimension of the city, do yourself a favor and take in some of its other shrines.

St. Joseph's Oratory (3800 Queen Mary, just west of Côte des Neiges, tel: 733-8211; Metro: Côte des Neiges) was founded by Brother André, whose miraculous works are attested to by the collection of discarded crutches and wheelchairs that belonged to those he is credited with curing. Tour buses usually pass the Oratory, whose spectacular dome dominates the northwestern slope of *Mount Royal*, but many visitors neglect to enter the Museum of the Oratory or the chapel. Modeled on St. Peter's Basilica in Rome, St. Joseph's boasts the world's third-largest dome (after St. Peter's and a massive cathedral constructed by Felix

Houphouet-Boigny in Côte d'Îvoire). Several events take place in the Oratory year round, including organ recitals, chorals, and, of course, masses. Guided tours are available daily at 13:30 from 24 June to 4 September. The Carillon, which was built in France and originally intended for the Eiffel Tower, plays Wednesday through Sunday at noon, Wednesday to Friday at 15:00, and Saturday and Sunday at 14:30. At night, the view from the top of the Oratory's vast outdoor staircase is breathtaking, and because the edifice is closed then you won't have to share the experience with a throng. Facing the Oratory across Queen Mary is the Collège Notre Dame (3791 Queen Mary). A plaque and bas-relief mark the door at which Brother André served as a humble porter. **36**

St. Enfant Jésus (5039 St. Dominique, just south of Laurier; Metro: Laurier) dates from 1858. Nicknamed the wedding-cake church for its resemblance to an ornamental cake top, it is a beautifully crafted structure. Once the centerpiece of the village of St. Louis de Mile End, it serves as a reminder of the grand projects once undertaken by the different municipalities that competed with Montreal for supremacy of the island (another such Mile End landmark is the fire station one block west at the corner of St. Laurent and Laurier; it now houses the *Musée des Pompiers Auxiliaires de Montréal*). In seasons when tours are not offered, the church may be entered during mass, as long as your visit is discrete and doesn't disturb the worshippers. Tours are offered Wednesday to Sunday 10:00 to 17:00 during the summer only. **57**

Inaugurated in 1865 by the Jesuits as the chapel of the Collège Sainte Marie, the **Gésu** (1202 Bleury, south of Ste. Catherine West; Metro: Place des Arts) is one of the oldest churches in the city. The frescoes are done in the Baroque trompe-l'oeil style. The

church is most renowned for its masterful marquetry. It is open daily from 07:00 to 17:15, except Sunday afternoon. Visitors are welcome to view the church, but as this is first a church, and second an attraction, they are asked to respect worshippers. Beneath the chapel is the **Salle du Gésu** a wonderfully intimate concert venue that often hosts jazz shows. 🔢

Église Très Saint Sacrement (500 Mont Royal East, just east of St. Denis; Metro: Mont Royal) is the first church of the Très Saint Sacrement in North America. It was completed in 1892, and declared a historic monument in 1975. After the structure was ravaged by fire in 1984 it was restored. It is located in the heart of the *Plateau Mont Royal*, just down the street from the district's *Maison de la Culture.* 🔢

S E C R E T

RESTAURANTS
(GENERAL)

English writer Samuel Butler, who visited Montreal from August 1874 until the end of 1875, commented on the food to be found in the city: "When the Canadians have a decent restaurant, they will be a nicer people, and when they are a nicer people they will have a decent restaurant." On this criteria, Montrealers must now rank as among the nicest people in the world. One would be hard-pressed to think of an ethnic cuisine that is not well represented. Any type of food that tempts your palate is to be found, and, with few exceptions, it may be enjoyed at most any time of day or night.

Montrealers share with Parisians a particular fondness for eating outdoors. Many restaurants feature a terrace during the summer, and some that don't merely spill tables out onto the street at their doorstep. If you prefer dining indoors, at least take a break at one of the multitude of cafés with terraces and watch the people going by.

A comprehensive listing of Montreal's eateries would demand a book all its own, and indeed, many such books exist. Here we will direct you to establishments with a particularly storied pedigree, and with a particular focus on the variety of ethnic cuisine the city boasts.

Vieux St. Gabriel (426 St. Gabriel in *Old Montreal*, tel: 878-3561) is the oldest inn in North America, established in 1754. The beautiful stone-walled interior is adorned with many artifacts from the French colonial period. In 1769, it was the first establishment granted a liquor licence by the British. For a less expensive alternative with the same ambiance, try the adjoining **Pub St. Gabriel** (420 St. Gabriel) for a drink.

Enjoy dinner inside Montreal's old women's prison at **Ancre d'Or** (777 de la Commune West, near McGill, tel: 875-5162).

Exotika (400 Laurier West, just west of du Parc, tel: 273-5015) offers more than just a meal in the restaurant, coffee in the café cum magazine/CD store, or a drink in the lounge — it promises the novelty of escape. The decor intends to simulate travel, to bring you into the lush, welcome shelter of a safari camp in the middle of Africa. Yet, for all its foreign decor, it is strangely homey.

The eclectic menu reflects a global outlook, including such dishes as alligator, paella, ostrich, steaks, fish, stingray, and teryaki, among others. Brunch is served on weekends, and the lounge features live music Thursday through Sunday. If you're alone and looking for a place for coffee, light lunch, or dessert, sit at the counter of the ground-floor café where each place is fitted with headphones and a selection of CDs for your private listening. Forget to bring reading material? Magazines are on sale.

S E C R E T

RETRO CLOTHING

The human race has had centuries to dream up every possible fashion variation. So, inevitably, everything old becomes new again — what once was banished to the back of the closet earns a second life as vintage apparel. Along a stretch of **Mont Royal East** between St. Laurent and St. Hubert in the *Plateau Mont Royal* district you'll find a concentration of funky and quirky second-hand clothing stores unmatched elsewhere in the city. A close inspection could unearth some unique item at an impossible-to-pass-up price. In any event, the effort will be fun (Metro: Mont Royal).

Twist Encore (3972 St. Laurent, south of Duluth, tel: 842-1308) stands apart from the Mont Royal strip, but offers the same sort of wares. Worth the visit if you're a used-clothing hound.

Boutique Sheilagh (346A Victoria, in Westmount, south of Sherbrooke, tel: 484-8805; Metro: Vendôme) specializes in nearly new designer fashions. All stock is in excellent condition. Prices are high by second-hand standards, but, given the quality of the labels the shop carries, there are bargains to be had.

Boutique Fantasque (2080 Crescent, tel: 288-3655; Metro: Guy-Concordia) is yet another lightly used designer-label emporium.

SECRET
SANDWICHES

Café Santropol (3990 St. Urbain, corner of Duluth, tel: 842-3110) serves up big, sprouty sandwiches in a worn, somewhat seedy Bohemian atmosphere. The menu includes selections for vegetarians and nonvegetarians alike. If you can't get enough outdoor dining while the warm weather lasts, come here on a cold day and dine outside surrounded by heat lamps.

Welcome to the asylum. The bizarre staff at **Terrasse Elgin** (1100 Docteur Penfield, corner of Stanley, tel: 849-6411) don't seem to have much of a clue, so don't be surprised if, while you're eating, the waiter passes by with a spray can of air freshener. And don't be discouraged if the staff seems utterly uninterested in taking your order. Once someone does, you're in for a superb sandwich stuffed into fresh pita. This little restaurant, tucked away inside an apartment tower, is known only to McGill University types and those living in the building itself.

Le Club Sandwich (1578 Ste. Catherine East, east of Amherst, tel: 523-4679) is open for business 24 hours a day.

SECRET

SKATING

Budget cuts have caused the city to reduce the number of outdoor rinks they maintain, but the best remain intact. **Beaver Lake** (Lac aux Castors) on *Mount Royal* and **Parc Lafontaine** (most easily reached by taking Sherbrooke east past St. Denis, where it will be found on the north side of the street) are among the most enchanting. Further east is the **Parc Maisonneuve** rink (also accessible from Sherbrooke East, at Viau, past the *Olympic Stadium*). Others are at the **Old Port** (*Old Montreal*), at the old Olympic rowing basin on **Île Notre Dame**, and at **Île Ste. Hélène** (both accessible from the Parc des Îles exit off the Jacques Cartier Bridge). Few outdoor rinks offer skate rentals, so bring your own.

Amphitheatre Bell (1000 de la Gauchetière West, corner of University, tel: 395-0555; Metro: Bonaventure) has an indoor rink, open daily 11:30 to 22:00. Admission $5. Skate rentals are available.

SECRET
SKIING

Though Montrealers flock to the Laurentians and Eastern Townships to cross-country ski on more challenging, undulating terrain (not to mention to flee the city for a day), there are several trails within the city limits for those who are loathe to waste time in the car.

The **Morgan Arboretum** (Chemin Ste. Marie, Ste. Anne de Bellevue, tel: 398-7811; take Highway 40 West, exit 41) offers peaceful, heavily wooded trails. Note that access is restricted to Friends of the Arboretum on weekends in January and February. Adults $4, children and seniors $2, families $10.

Parc Angrignon (Boulevard des Trinitaires, Lasalle, tel: 872-3066 or 872-6211) has two trails.

Mount Royal is ribboned with trails. However, unless you go during the week or very early on weekends, don't expect any sense of solitude.

Parcs *Lafontaine* and *Maisonneuve* also offer cross-country skiing, as does *Île. Ste. Hélène* (tel: 872-6093).

S E C R E T

SMOKES

Although cigarette smokers may have fallen to a social strata once reserved for carriers of infectious disease, cigar smokers have achieved trendsetter status. Nothing beats sitting under an aromatic pall of thick smoke, I suppose. Go figure.

American visitors can enjoy the joint pleasures of puffing a good cigar and committing an illicit act by indulging in a fine Cuban stogie. These forbidden Castro exports can be found at any decent tobacconist.

Henri Poupart (1385 Ste. Catherine West, between Bishop and Crescent, tel: 842-5794; Metro: Guy-Concordia) is the oldest cigar emporium in Montreal, with one of the finest selections of imported tobacco products. In a very utilitarian design, everything is laid out behind the counter.

Brand new to this location, **Davidoff** (1452 Sherbrooke West, just west of the Montreal Museum of Fine Arts, tel: 289-9118; Metro: Guy-Concordia) is the kind of shop one pictures while leafing through the pages of *Cigar Afficionado*. Step into the walk-in humidor to be engulfed by the scent of fine tobacco. Offering an excellent selection of smokes and associated accoutrements, this store will make a nonsmoker yearn to take up the habit.

La Casa del Habano (1434 Sherbrooke West, west of Crescent, tel: 849-0037; Metro: Guy-Concordia) basks in the comfortable decadence that is the essence of enjoying a fine cigar. The two walk-in humidors at the front of the shop offer a selection fit for the true connoisseur. At the back is a lounge where you're welcome to repair to indulge in a relaxing, leisurely smoke. Sink into a deep leather chair and take pleasure in stimulating companionship or quiet contemplation. The lounge is accessible during regular store hours, daily from 10:00 to 18:00, Thursday and Friday until 21:00.

Most of the more elegant clubs on Crescent, St. Denis, and St. Laurent streets permit cigar smoking in deference to the fad. **Allegra Cigar Lounge** (3523 St. Laurent, in the heart of the nightlife strip from Sherbrooke north to Prince Arthur) simply happens to be the trendiest of the trendy. Expect to wait in line on weekends unless you arrive unfashionably early. Most of the sunglasses-at-night crowd would rather spend an hour outside in the dead of winter than show up too soon. Wear black or stand out.

SECRET
SOCCER

Perhaps less hidden than ignored, pro soccer has had several incarnations in Montreal. The most recent is the **Impact** (for info, call 328-3668), the 1995 North American A-League champions. They play home games at the modest **Centre Claude Robillard** (1000 Émile Journault, tel: 872-6911).

SECRET
SUGAR SHACKS

The *cabane à sucre* is a Québécois tradition celebrating the spring thaw that sets free the sap from maple trees, allowing for the production of our world-famous maple syrup. The season is roughly from March through April, but varies from year to year. As with fruit and vegetable picking, the ***Monterégie*** and ***Laurentides*** have the greatest concentration of cabanes in close proximity to Montreal. Several Monterégie cabanes are located in Mont St. Grégoire, St. Stanislas de Kostka, Ste. Julie, and St. Marc sur Richelieu, while Mirabel and St. Eustache have the highest concentration of shacks in the *Laurentides*. Call the appropriate tourism office (Monterégie, 514-674-5555; Laurentides, 514-436-8532 or 800-561-6673) for exact locations and seasonal information. ⓲ ㉒

Open all year, the **Sucrerie de la Montagne** (300 St. Georges, Rigaud, tel: 514-451-5204) is the most famous of the cabanes. The huge log-cabin dining room sits atop Mont Rigaud in the Monterégie. Folk singers and dancers in traditional garb entertain during your meal of eggs, ham, bacon, potatoes, beans, and créton (fried fat, an acquired taste), all smothered in maple syrup. The only thing not smothered in maple syrup, in fact, is the sinfully sweet sugar pie they serve for dessert. Check your arteries at the door and dig in. ⓿

SECRET
SWIMS

⚜

In case your hotel doesn't have its own pool and you're in need of a refreshing dip, try one of the following venues.

Bain Morgan (1875 Morgan, north of Notre Dame East in *Hochelaga-Maisonneuve*, tel: 872-6657) is a functional example of the old public baths on which Montrealers once depended for cleanliness more than recreation. (An exhibit at the *Écomusée du Fier Monde* explores the history of this city's public baths.) While most of the old baths have fallen into disuse or been destroyed, this grand beaux-arts building is now an indoor swimming pool. It also hosts periodic exhibitions. Bain Morgan is situated on a beautiful street named for the founder of a huge Montreal department store (now a dilapidated hulk at Mansfield and Ste. Catherine).

At the south end of the street is a lovely park (Parc Morgan), which used to be the site of Morgan's great chateau. Continue strolling up Morgan, to the corner of Hochelaga, and you'll reach the *Marché Maisonneuve*, one of Montreal's outdoor markets. The grand domed building, currently a *Maison de la Culture*, housed the original market.

Centre Aquatique Rivière des Prairies (12725 Rodolphe For-get, in the northeast district of Rivière des Prairies, tel: 872-9322) is a welcoming indoor family-swimming center, with three pools: one with a deep end, a shallower one for younger swimmers, and a wading pool for toddlers. It also has three changing rooms: the usual male and female, and a third where parents of either sex can assist their young children. A nice atmosphere for a family outing.

Hôtel de la Montagne (1430 de la Montagne, between Ste. Catherine West and de Maisonneuve West, tel: 288-5656; Metro: Peel) has a very popular terrace pool/bar on its roof, open during the summer only. Admission is open to those who are not guests of the hotel, but you must be 18 or over. There have been sightings of topless sunbathers here.

Hôtel Bonaventure (Place Bonaventure, de la Gauchetière west of University, tel: 878-2332; Metro: Bonaventure) has a tranquil outdoor pool, available even in the dead of winter. Set in a garden where pheasants roam, this heated year-round oasis is reason enough to book a room. Open to guests only.

Hôtel Westin Mont Royal (1050 Sherbrooke West, corner of Peel, tel: 284-1110; Metro: Peel) is the other place to book for an outdoor swim in winter. There's no better way to mock nature than to paddle serenely in warmth while everyone else walks around chilled to the bone. Guests only.

Okay, so maybe it's not what most people imagine when they think of the great outdoors, but **L'Octagone** (on Gouin, at Tanguay, in the far-west end of the city) offers a bar with a pool (or vice versa) on a terrace overlooking the Rivière des Prairies. It's a great place to laze away a summer afternoon. Directly across the street is the brooding hulk of Bordeaux Jail. So raise a glass in a toast to your own glorious freedom.

SECRET
THEATER

Every summer, **Repercussion Theatre** (tel: 485-6000) presents Shakespeare in the Park, an enchanting evening of Shakespeare performed under the stars in a variety of suburban parks, including those found in Westmount, Outremont, Montreal West, Côte St. Luc, and Town of Mount Royal. All of these locations are easily accessible from the center of town. The plays provide a good excuse to visit some decidedly un-touristy neighborhoods (in some instances, you may well be the only out-of-towner). Though the quality of the performances can vary from year to year, they are most often quite good. Bring your own blanket or lawn chair to the performance, or else find yourself sitting on the bare grass. Call for information on the play, location, dates, and times.

Théâtre Espace GO (5066 Clark, near Laurier, tel: 271-0813; Metro: Laurier) is a women's theater that produces plays by women.

McGill boasts a variety of theatrical offerings. The Department of English stages two major productions a year. Details can be obtained by calling 398-6558 or 398-6577. The **Tuesday Night Café Theatre** runs year-round at Morrice Hall. For scheduling info, call 398-6600. **Player's Theatre** is a student-run group that mounts plays in the Shatner Student Union Building (3480 McTavish, north of Sherbrooke, Metro: Peel). Call for info at 398-6813.

Black Theatre Workshop is an active independent company that produces a range of works. For all the details, call 932-1104.

S E C R E T

THEATRICALS

Grotesque gargoyles outside the **La Divine Comédie** (1037 Bleury, corner of de la Gauchetière, tel: 392-9268) ward off unwanted intruders. For years, the owners of this calculatedly dilapidated and dreary building have battled city officials who consider the structure more eyesore than work of art. The theme of this restaurant/theater only recently changed from a haunted house — where dinner was presided over by a variety of evil spirits, long-deceased historical characters, vampires, and other ghouls — to a recreation of the beauty of Dante's *Divine Comedy*. In keeping with this new spirit, the side of the building has now been adorned with a jollier assortment of characters. Last time I attended, it was evident that the emphasis was more on the show than the meal, but the menu has since been expanded. Currently, the restaurant/theater is open only for lunch (11:00 to 14:30). The haunted-house experience is presented most Friday and Saturday nights, but you must be part of a group of at least 10 people (there are no such restrictions for the *Divine Comedy* show).

SECRET

WALKS

The **Société Historique de Montréal** (headquartered at 462 Place Jacques Cartier, in *Old Montreal*, tel: 878-9008) hosts walking tours of *Chinatown*, which lies just north of *Old Montreal*, in the sector from Viger north to René Lévesque, and St. Laurent east to Clark. The tours, which cost $35, strive to incorporate the historic, the cultural, and the gastronomic — many of the hidden spots of the district are pointed out, and a meal is included. The tours are conducted primarily in French, but many of the guides are bilingual and can accommodate English participants. Conducted weekly between May and October, the tours are very popular with locals, so call ahead to confirm the schedule and to reserve a place.

Heritage Montréal (1181 de la Montagne, tel: 875-2985) is a private foundation dedicated to developing and promoting Montreal's urban heritage. They organize two-hour walking tours every Saturday and Sunday afternoon, rain or shine, from June through September, led by knowledgeable guides with expertise in urban planning, local history, and architecture. The walks offer insightful explorations of well-known and less well-known sectors of the city, including parts of downtown, Pointe St. Charles, Notre Dame de Grâce, and Côte des Neiges, among others. The guides will point out architectural characteristics, cultural quirks, and the historical significance of areas under exploration. Not only will they introduce you to obscure pockets of Montreal, but they will also grant new perspectives on areas that might otherwise seem to have no hidden depths. Tours always begin and end at a metro station to maximize convenience. There is no advance registration; just show up at the designated corner on the appropriate day and pay on the spot ($8 per walk for nonmembers of Heritage Montréal). Interestingly, nearly every participant is a Montrealer. Tours are offered in both English and French; an advantage for anglophones is that the English tours have far fewer participants.

For those interested in the architecture of downtown and the fabled *Golden Square Mile*, Heritage Montréal offers **Architectours** (tel: 875-2985). Two separate walks are given: Dorchester Square (Fridays at 14:00) and the Square Mile (Saturdays at 14:00). They are provided in French and English and depart from the *Info Touriste* (1001 Dorchester Square). The two-hour walks are conducted rain or shine every week from late May until early October (call to confirm schedule). The price is $8.

For an alternative look at the social history of Montreal, participate in one of **L'Autre Montréal**'s two- to three-hour bus excursions. As the name implies (L'Autre Montréal means "the other Montreal"), these tours promise to show a side of the city overlooked by standardized, *official* tours. Based on original research undertaken by the group's members, each tour offers a reality-based excursion that will expose you to the offbeat and the gritty. Animated by stories of the characters that contributed to (or sometimes detracted from) Montreal's development, these tours present a history of place that isn't necessarily tied down to a specific architectural monument. The group conducts a variety of tours in French. In 1996, for the first time, they did two tours in English: "Women in the City: The Contribution of Women to

Montreal's History," and "Hochelaga-Maisonneuve: An In-depth Look at Montreal's East End." Due to the interest expressed by the English community, a more extensive schedule is anticipated for 1997. Among the French tours are explorations of intercultural Montreal, the environment, social justice and democracy (this tour involves costumed role-players), and urban development. They depart at 10:00 on Sundays, between June and October, from Carré St. Louis at St. Denis. The cost is $12. For more information, contact L'Autre Montreal by phone at 521-7802, or post at 2138 Rachel East, Montreal, Quebec H2H 1P9.

The **Jewish Public Library** (5151 Côte Ste. Catherine, tel: 345-2629) sponsors **Summer Walking Tours of Historic and Literary Jewish Montreal**. Led by the eminently qualified teacher, filmmaker, and writer Stanley Asher, these walks shed light on the rich contribution of the Jewish community to Montreal. Because Jews were among the earliest immigrants to the city, the walks take you through some of the older sections of the *Plateau Mont Royal* and the Main. Highlights include early synagogues, many of which have been converted to churches or schools, the first schools attended by Jews, and sites associated with authors Leonard Cohen, Irving Layton, and Mordecai Richler. There is a series of three two-hour walks, costing $3 each, or $7 for the series. In 1996 they occurred on successive Sundays in August. For further details, contact the Jewish Public Library.

Among the activities organized by the **Société d'Histoire d'Outremont** (tel: 935-1548) is a series of four walks that explore the history of Montreal's Outremont quarter ($8 each for non-members, $20 for all four). They run on consecutive weekends, from late August to early September (call for the current schedule).

Several walking tours of the **Plateau Mont Royal** are offered through the summer and fall. **Guidatour** (tel: 844-4021 or 800-363-4021) arranges outings from late June through September. **Amarage** (tel: 272-7049) offers walks that discuss the multi-ethnic character of the Plateau, as well as one that focuses on the Portuguese community. Call for current schedules.

Among the many programs sponsored by the ***Canadian Centre for Architecture*** (tel: 439-7026) are several walks over weekends in October through the parks and gardens of Montreal. Those on Mount Royal are offered in conjunction with the Centre de la Montagne (tel: 844-4928), while others, including the parks of Outremont and Westmount and the grounds of the Grand Seminaire, are hosted by Heritage Montréal (tel: 875-2985).

Mohawk Trail Tours (tel: 635-7289) guides walking tours of *Kahnawake*, the Mohawk territory just south of Montreal, across the Mercier Bridge. Explaining the culture and history of the Mohawk people, a guide will lead you to the major points of interest on the territory and through the streets of the old village. The walks are held as long as weather permits on Friday, Saturday, and Sunday from 10:00 to 12:00. The walk costs $16 ($13 for students and golden age, $7.50 for children 6–14, or $45 for a family of four). For an additional $10, you can get transportation to and from downtown (the meeting point is the northwest corner of Peel and de la Gauchetière, at 09:15).

THE SECRET FUTURE

No tour guide can be definitively comprehensive, especially when the aim is to uncover those hidden places that have previously escaped notice. Undoubtedly, some worthwhile attractions have remained hidden even from our best efforts to ferret them out.

In the interest of our own self-improvement, we ask readers to let us know of the places they've unearthed that they believe warrant inclusion in future editions of *Secret Montreal*. If we use your suggestion, we'll send you a free copy on publication. Please contact us at the following address:

Secret Montreal
c/o ECW PRESS
2120 Queen Street East, Suite 200
Toronto, ON M4E 1E2

Or e-mail us at: ECW@SYMPATICO.CA

SUBJECT INDEX

MAP INDEX

EASTERN DOWNTOWN

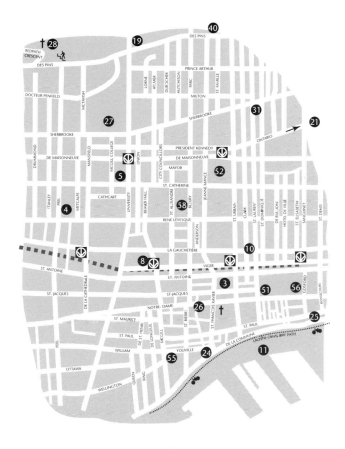

WESTERN DOWNTOWN

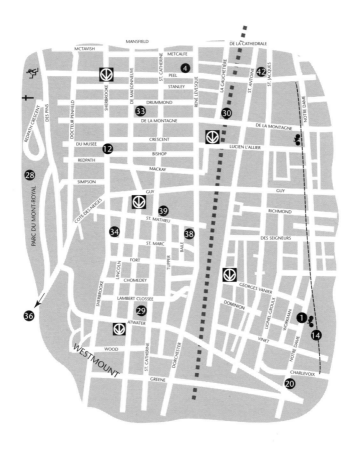

N

PLATEAU MONT ROYAL

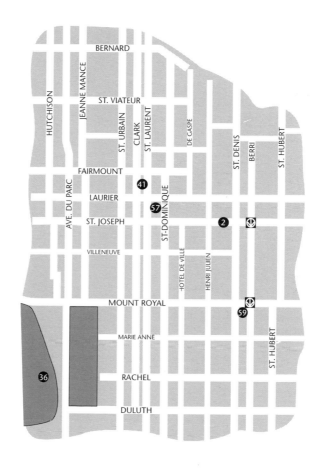

HOCHELAGA-MAISONNEUVE

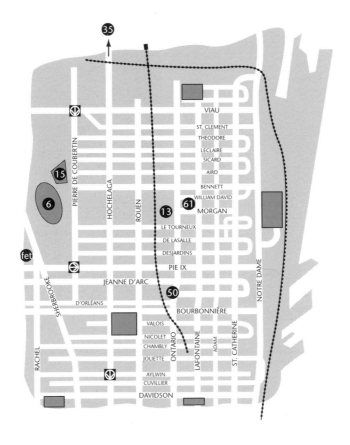

AROUND THE EDGES

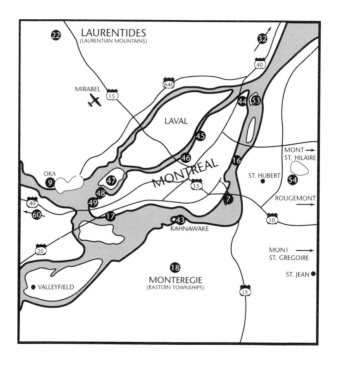